Top Secret!

Top Secret!

A Complete and Powerful Business Guide
for Salon Professionals.

Jeanne Degen

POSITIVE
SALON
STRATEGIES

www.PositiveSalonStrategies.com

DEDICATION

I dedicate this book to my friends and family for all their encouragement, love and support throughout the years.

CONTENTS

ACKNOWLEDGEMENTS

I would like to acknowledge Mimi McCarthy for all her contributions in writing this book, Emmy Intoppa for all the research and efforts put into creating this book, and Richard W. Huntley Jr. for the endless hours put into editing this book to make it a success.

CHAPTER ONE

THE ABC'S OF OPERATING YOUR SALON

THE ABC'S OF OPERATING YOUR SALON
SECTION ONE

DEVELOPING DISCIPLINE FOR DOLLAR$

In today's economic climate, it is all about outshining your competition, isn't it? It's all about establishing a strategy that sets you apart and makes you different. The fact is, salon professionals cannot only excel in the art and science of the beauty profession; they must also excel in the business side of the industry as well.

In this chapter, *The ABC's of Operating Your Salon*, you will learn how to re-motivate yourself as a salon owner.

We will cover how to keep your expenses under control.

You will learn how to create attainable, written goals that are easy to track.

We will discuss the importance of having a Point of Sale (POS) system in your salon.

We will review how to define your strengths and weaknesses and learn how to use this information to create a business action plan.

We will discuss the art of advertising.

We will discuss tips for hiring and retaining loyal staff, and much more.

Once you have completed the first section, you will see that the next sections will continue to build on the information we have already learned.

I have broken it down this way to make large amounts of information more manageable and to help simplify the process. You will want to keep a record of the information we cover as we progress through the trainings so that you have it to look back on and refer to. So let's get started!

In this first section, I want you to start off with identifying the areas in which your salon needs improvement.

Take as much time as you need to answer these questions, because the answers are important in order for you to be able to identify accurately the areas that you may need to change.

First, think back to the time when you were deciding to become a salon owner. Write down as many things as you can remember.

What motivated you in the first place to start a business of your own? For example, was it more free time? Were you looking to be your own boss? Or perhaps it was for investment or retirement purposes. This exercise will help you to re-establish the reasons you went into business in the first place.

_____

_____

_____

_____

What is the ultimate goal for your salon now? The best way to answer this question is by starting with your hoped-for end result because this will help you make a plan of action to build your business to achieve your goals. For example, I want my salon to make me a millionaire so I can have an early retirement.

_____

_____

_____

_____

Jot down some thoughts about what you feel would help you achieve your goals. We will delve into how to set written goals later on in this chapter, but for the moment, what do you think could motivate you to achieve your goals?

_____

_____

_____

_____

Has your experience as an owner been positive, or more trying? Take a few minutes to reflect on this question. It is always helpful to write things down, so make a list of what you have liked, and what you have not liked, about being an owner. For example, I enjoy working with my stylists. I like being my own boss. It has given me more time with my family. I like the freedom it allows me.

My experience as an owner has been···

List the positive things about your salon. For example, I have a fabulous staff. My salon is always presentable and at its best for every client that comes through the door. We pride ourselves on our outstanding customer service, etc.

List the areas where you feel improvement is needed. For example, my retail sales are very weak. I can' t seem to get my stylists to up-sell to their clientele. My revenue sales have dropped off since the recession, etc.

_____

_____

_____

_____

We will refer back to all this information later on in this chapter. First, however, it is time to probe a little deeper.

The next seven questions will help you to identify the strengths and weaknesses in your salon so you can create a plan to accentuate your strengths and to work on your weaknesses. We want to turn your salon's weaknesses into strengths.

1. Do you know what your breakeven is? In other words, do you know how much money your salon needs to generate before you make a profi Let's say your breakeven amount (the total dollar amount of all your expenses) is $10,000 per month. This is the amount you will need to bring in just to pay your bills. If you know your breakeven amount, enter it here: _____. If you don't know (or are unsure of) your breakeven amount, use the example "Profi and Loss Statement" on page 21 to calculate your breakeven amount and then enter that fi   in the space above.

2. Is your payroll in control? Are you paying more than 45% to your stylists? (This percentage would include your total payroll, salary, and/or commissions but exclude payroll taxes). A good rule of thumb to follow is that your payroll should be between 40-45% of your total revenue each week. For example, if your salon's total weekly revenue is $2,000, and you stay between the recommended percentage (the average of which is 43%), your payroll would be $860. Compute that number by multiplying your weekly revenue ($2,000) by 0.43 (43%) for an answer of $860. I have seen too many salons fail due to overpaying staff that the salon cannot afford. Overstaffi will cut into the salon's profi in a big way. Scheduling within your budgetary constraints is very important, especially if you are paying hourly rates and commission fees.

My weekly payroll is:_____.%

Many salons find it difficult to maintain control over their payroll cost, so consider these suggestions:

- Monitor non-technical people on your payroll

- Look at scheduling – are you overstaffing?

- Overtime should be controlled!

- Send people home in slow times

- Offer specials for the slower times of day

- Increase your retail and up-selling sales because these sales will increase your revenue without a big increase in payroll costs

- Remember, the most critical reasons why labor costs are not controlled are due to not training your staff properly, not scheduling your staff properly and not being able to retain team members. These are subjects we will continue to discuss further throughout this book.

I cannot emphasize strongly enough how important these exercises are; it is crucial to know these figures in order to keep your expenses intact. I know many people avoid the task of working through these numbers because it bores them, but it is an essential task for you to complete for your business to be a success.

I have worked with salon owners over the years who did not want to take the time to work through these questions, and time and again, they have told me later they wish they could go back and do it now. So please hang in there with me while we work through these questions.

3. Is your rent too high? If your salon is paying more than 10% of your total monthly revenue on rent, this could present a financial problem. For example, if your total revenue sales are $20,000 per month, then your rent should not exceed $2,000 ($20,000 x 0.10 = $2,000). In this current economy, landlords may be more willing to negotiate rental pricing in order to keep their property leased. I got my landlord to drop my lease $1,000 per month. Hey, it doesn't hurt to ask. My monthly rent is_____.

4. Is your electric bill too high? I cut my bill in half by purchasing a lock box with a key that only my manager and I had access to. This stopped the rest of the staff from setting the thermostat on a whim.

I also had it programmed to go off at night and back on in the morning. It made such a huge difference in the amount of my electric bill.

5. Do you know where your waste is? Waste is another common problem that can put a salon into serious debt. Over the years, I have witnessed stylists mixing up excess color only to throw half of it down the sink.

One way to keep on top of this would be to look at how many color services you are doing in a week.

For example, let' s say your stylists, on average, use a 2-ounce tube of color for every color service, and your cost for a 2-ounce tube of color is $5. If your salon averages 20 colors a week, then you are averaging 20 tubes of color a week. 20 tubes of color x $5 per tube = $100 of color per week. That should be your cost. If it is much more than that, you have a waste problem.

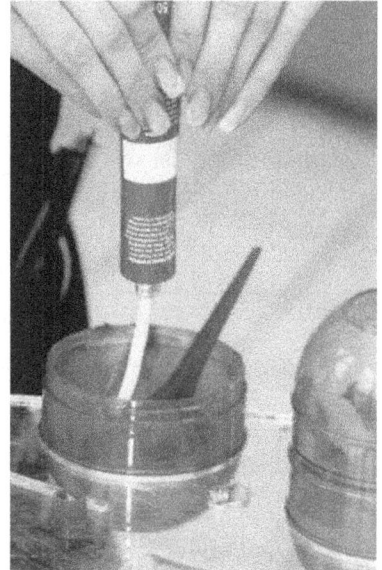

There are a number of steps you can take to decrease your color waste. Many salons overstock on color. Keep in mind that a salon should only stock 2-3 tubes of all colors and 4-6 tubes of frequently-used colors at one time.

If you haven' t done so already:

- You need a system for opened tubes,

- You should educate stylists on how to use color to make colors,

- Don' t allow your stylists to waste color or developer by not putting caps back on tightly.

Remember that waste can eventually cause huge profit loss.

6. Is your inventory in control? When ordering supplies, keep in mind you will need to establish a two-week ordering cycle and avoid small orders. Ideally, you should sell the last bottle of shampoo just as the truck delivers the next order.

You don' t want to overstock too much inventory because this, too, can cause a loss of profit, so try to order what you are sure you will sell. Remember, sending products back to the warehouse is costly because there is a restocking fee.

Conducting regular inventory is important and will let you know what product is moving and what product is not moving. Regular inventories will also help prevent theft. A good way to track your inventory is by using a Point of Sale system. (We will discuss POS systems in more detail later). You might consider some of these ideas to help you to move excess product:

- Use marketing tools to promote the sale of slower moving items

- Hold a sidewalk sale

- Put together value-added programs

- Make a basket containing your slow-moving products and hold a raffle

To avoid product loss that you cannot account for, train team members to track and control inventory through your computer and take weekly physical counts of all inventory – your staff will take notice.

7. Has your salon ever experienced theft? I have spoken to many salon owners over the years about theft from both staff and clients. In my own salons, I experienced my stylists not checking a client into the computer and taking the money from the client for themselves (this is yet another crucial reason to have a POS system in your salon, which we will cover later).

Voiding out legitimate sales, misuse of coupons, discounts, and gift certificates will all hurt salon profit. When a stylist gives free items or services to friends, relatives, or other team members using the salon's products, this will cut profit. You will find yourself ordering unnecessary inventory.

In my own salon experiences and while working with other salon owners, so many times I have heard the same story: the stylist always has an excuse such as she is not making enough money, or she works harder than anyone else in the salon, and therefore, she feels entitled. I have also heard stylists just blatantly deny it. It always amazes me how much this theft scenario occurs, and stylists often don't think of it as stealing.

If you are experiencing theft, or think you may be, I would highly suggest installing surveillance cameras. The cost for a whole camera system has gone down a great deal over the past few years. This immediately solved my problem with staff theft, and when I posted a sign that cameras were on the premise, it stopped clients as well from taking products. You can view the camera's recordings from your home or when you travel. It is a method to consider implementing to deter stealing and also to provide evidence if a theft does occur.

Now, after you have answered these questions, you need to be able to see what you are paying OUT in expenses versus what your salon is bringing IN. Obviously, this is crucial information to know.

One way to do this is to make a profit and loss list, with all of your expenses listed together and then your revenue, listed as well.

For example, your expenses will include things such as phone, electric, heat, cable, insurance costs, and so on. Your payroll, which is one of your expenses, will fluctuate as your salon grows. But for now, enter your current payroll expense. Your income, on the other hand, will include the money coming in to your salon; for example, revenue from selling your services as well as your products. If you don't already have a method to calculate profit and loss, use the tables on the following pages.

PROFIT AND LOSS STATEMENT

Monthly Expenses

Expenses	JAN	FEB	MAR	APR	MAY	JUNE	JULY	AUG	SEPT	OCT	NOV	DEC
Payroll, Wages, Payroll Taxes, etc												
Debt Loans												
Advertising												
Credit Card Fee												
Product & Sundries												
Bank Charges												
Insurance												
POS Charge												
Miscellaneous												
Licenses												
Office Expenses												
Electric												
Gas												
Phone												
Cable/Internet												
Training & Seminars												
Rent												
Repairs & Maintenance												
Uniform/Clothing												
Other												
TOTAL MONTHLY EXPENSES												

Monthly Sales

Sales	JAN	FEB	MAR	APR	MAY	JUNE	JULY	AUG	SEPT	OCT	NOV	DEC
Service Sales												
Retail Sales												
TOTAL MONTHLY SALES												

Calculate Your Profit/Loss

	JAN	FEB	MAR	APR	MAY	JUNE	JULY	AUG	SEPT	OCT	NOV	DEC
Total Monthly Sales												
- Total Monthly Expenses												
PROFIT/LOSS:												

You should update this profit and loss list on a monthly basis so you can keep close tabs on how much money is coming in and how much is going out. Anything you make above your breakeven amount (which, again, is the total of all your monthly expenses) is *profit!*

Now that you have some actual figures in front of you and you have answered the important questions we discussed, we need to look at how to improve and grow your business internally.

The next step is to complete the following "Salon Evaluation Worksheet" exercise on the next four pages to determine your salon's strengths and weaknesses. This is the place where you can utilize the information about your strengths and weaknesses that your wrote down at the beginning of this chapter.

SALON EVALUATION WORKSHEET

Directions: Complete the following form to identify and outline the specific Plan of Action for your salon.

Date: _

Salon: _

Issue Description I: Check the category that best identifies "Needs Improvement."

	Salon Operations
	Increase of Customer Base
	Educational Needs
	Increase of Retail and Service Sales
	Overall Business Development/ In-salon and External Promotions/ Community and Small Business Net-Working

Issue Description II: Circle any boxes that best identify what needs solving.

Salon Operations	Day-to-Day Operations	Increase in Revenue	Customer Service	Staffing	Stylist Retention
Overall Business Development	Outside Promotions	In-Salon Promotions (Staff)	Community Marketing	Cross Promotions	In-Salon Promotions (Client)
Client Needs	New Clients	Repeat Clients	Walk-Outs	Re-do Services	Client Growth
Retail Needs	Sales	Inventory	Product Usage	Back Bar Waste	Team Efforts
Education Needs	Technical Training	Soft Skill Training	New Trends	Product Knowledge	Staff Issues

If Education/Training is required, please define:

Technical Education	Soft Skill Education

Networking Exercise (Check all that are within a 5-mile radius of your salon)

	Wal-Mart, Lowes, Home Depot, or other similar large stores
	Malls
	Nail Salons
	Workout Centers
	Senior Activity Centers
	Retail (Clothing)
	Churches
	Colleges
	High Schools/Junior High Schools
	Restaurants
	Independent Salons and Spas
	Grocery Stores
	Tanning Salons
	Weight Watchers/Curves (or similar)
	Other:

Are you currently running promotions with any of the above?	Yes	No
If "Yes," please list:		

In-Salon Promotion Exercise

List all Current *In-Salon* Promotions	
List all Current *External Salon* Discounts/Coupons	

	Yes	No
Do you currently have an e-mail mailing list?	Yes	No
Do you currently have a Customer Loyalty Program?	Yes	No
Do you currently have a salon newsletter?	Yes	No
Are you currently hosti any special events?	Yes	No

Question	Always	Sometimes	Never
Salon staff provides good customer service.			
Salon staff up-sells services.			
Salon staff up-sells retail.			
Salon experiences walk-out clients.			
Salon experiences re-do services.			
Salon is well-staffed.			
Salon staff has professional appearance.			
Salon holds staff meetings.			
Salon is clean and organized.			

Overall Evaluation

Salon Strengths	Salon Weaknesses
1.	1.
2.	2.
3.	3.
4.	4.
5.	5.

Listed on the next page are various salon topics. Read through the list and check the space that best indicates the priority in which your salon needs support in that area.

Topic	Low Priority	Medium Priority	High Priority
Client Retention			
New Clients			
Increase of Retail Sales			
Internal Staff Problems			
Customer Service Improvement			
Technical Training			
Staff Recruitment			
Salon and Staff Image			
In-Salon Promotions			
Training for Management			
Up-selling Services			
Team Member Mentality			
Community Promotions			
Goal Setting			
Inventory Control			
Marketing/Advertising			
Waste Control			
Other:			

Technical Training Needed:

Additional Education Needed:

List the Top 3 Needs For Your Salon:	1.
	2.
	3.

In Section 3 of this chapter, I provide many great ideas to help you strengthen the weaknesses you've just identified in this worksheet. However, before we delve into solutions, it is critical for you **first** to set goals for your salon and staff. The information you have been gathering and writing down in this section will help you to develop a clear understanding of what your salon needs to succeed. With this information in mind, we will learn how to set goals and then how to actually implement a plan to make those goals a reality in your salon. With the bulk of the financial work behind us, I can begin sharing with you so many proven strategies to get you on track!

THE ABC'S OF OPERATING YOUR SALON

SECTION TWO

SETTING AND ACHIEVING YOUR GOALS

In this second section of *The ABC's of Operating Your Salon*, we will learn the importance of setting written goals and then we will look at how to execute the proper steps to achieve a positive outcome.

First, let me ask you a question. Are you working <u>in </u>your business or <u>on </u>your business?

If you are working in your business, and you are a licensed cosmetologist, you are probably working behind the chair. This will bring in money, but it will impose limitations on you and your time, which will negatively impact your ability to run a successful business. You must balance your time between working in your salon and working on the business side of your salon.

You need to count on your staff to bring in most of your revenue. It is important that the owner invest most of his or her time running the salon.

It takes time and planning to be successful, and the owner should be developing game plans for the salon. What areas need improving? How am I going to improve them and put a plan in action? This is where the importance of a business plan comes in to play, and it all starts with goals. Setting goals for your salon and staff will allow you to keep track of your business at all times. It will also let you monitor how the salon and staff are performing, taking the guesswork out of evaluations.

Your goals must always be attainable, written, and easy to track.

In order to write your goals, you should identify your salon's uniqueness. Do you offer services that other salons don't offer, or do you offer services that other nearby salons offer as well?

_____

_____

_____

You must know your competition: Do they specialize in chemical services, kid's cuts, men's business, etc.?

_____

_____

_____

Knowing your competition allows you to determine how you will compete with your competition.

Try to focus on areas other than price. For example, you might offer a 100% money back guarantee.

This always sends the message to the client that you are secure that your services are of the highest quality.

After you have answered the questions above, gather that information together with all the information you just completed in Section One (financial information, "Salon Evaluation Worksheet," etc.). Now that you have determined the areas where you feel your salon can improve and the areas where your salon can succeed – in other words, you have researched your strengths/weaknesses, your finances, and your competition - you should have an idea of possible attainable goals for your salon. Don't forget to write your goals down!

Let's start off with some examples of a goal.

GOAL: I would like to double my hair cutting business within nine months.

You have defined an attainable goal and have given it a time frame.

Next you need to create an action plan that delivers your goal.

An example of the ACTION PLAN could be:

1. With every haircut, clients will receive a free sample-sized product of their choice.

2. We will create a loyalty stamp card for each client that states, after five haircuts, the sixth haircut is free.

Let me share another example of a creative action plan. A salon I worked with found their niche by advertising that they specialized in the expertise of cutting long hair. How many times have we heard the horror stories and complaints that a client asked the stylist to cut an inch and she took off three inches instead? As a result, many people with long hair won't get their hair cut on a regular basis. This salon made a killing in accentuating a service that many other salons were weak in. They tracked their business with a POS system, which is something I discuss in the next segment, and they tripled their business in six-month's time.

Another example of a GOAL may be: I want to increase my color business by 20 percent in the next six months.

Again, you have defined a specific goal and have given it a measurable time frame.

Now you need to write down an ACTION PLAN on how you plan to achieve this goal.

It may look like this.

1. Offer advanced color education for the staff.

2. Offer luncheon specials for the working woman. In this lunchtime special package, the client will get five-seven foils with her haircut and will receive a free, deep protein conditioner. You can offer snacks to make it even more inviting.

3. Put together events or incentives for your staff to up-sell a color service to clients who are scheduled for just a haircut.

4. Give a free bottle of shampoo when clients get a color service done.

5. Plan a color extravaganza day – this is a great way to build new color clients. You may want to offer 25-50% off your color services for new clients. Make sure you rebook them for their next appointment by offering them $5.00 off their next visit when they book that day.

This may sound expensive, but remember that a happy and content color client will become a loyal client, and loyal clients grow your bottom line. There are so many ideas you can come up with when you are writing your action plan to meet your goals that will separate you from your competition.

For example:

➤ Offer 5-minute massages and deep conditioning with every shampoo.

➢ Offer a wine and cheese after-hours for the working woman and man.

➢ Advertise a lunch special for the working woman: Get your nails and hair done while having lunch provided by the salon.

➢ Offer a pampering, moisturizing paraffin hand treatment while you get your hair done.

➢ Give out brochures listing all of your services to existing clients so that they can pass them out to friends.

➢ Have a "Children's Day" haircut program.

➢ Offer a "Try Me" special on your least-requested service, such as a complimentary deep protein treatment with every haircut.

➢ Offer a limited time "Bring a Friend" discount.

➢ Hold a "Mousse and Gel Clinic" in your salon to demonstrate spiking and scrunching methods.

➢ Think of a creative promotion for each and every holiday. Sound impossible? It's not.

➢ Offer a senior citizen's special.

➢ Pass out brochures at your local shopping mall.

➢ Start a salon newsletter.

In the next section, Section 3, you will find many more ideas that you can use when you are developing your action plans. Truly, the ideas are endless. Once you find your niche and your uniqueness, elaborate on it as much as possible!

When you are ready to start writing goals and action plans for your salon, I have included an easy-to-use "Salon Plan of Action" table on the next several pages for your convenience.

Salon Plan of Action

Write Your Goals and Action Plans

In-Salon Promotions *(Events/Extravaganzas)*
Goal:
Action Plan:

In-Salon Promotions *(Retail Promotions)*
Goal:
Action Plan:

In-Salon Promotions *(In-Salon Service Specials)*

Goal:

Action Plan:

Outside-Salon Promotions - Coupons/Discounts

Goal:

Action Plan:

	Outside-Salon Promotions - Community Marketing *(Promotions Within the Community)*
	Goal:
	Action Plan:

So we have talked about setting goals for your salon; now we need to look at goal setting with your stylists. In order to accurately set goals, you will need to communicate regularly with every stylist so that you can evaluate their overall performance.

For example, some questions you will want to ask are:

- What are the stylist's strengths?

- Where are the areas that need improvement?

- Does the stylist sell retail?

- Does the stylist up-sell services?

- Could the stylist improve his or her speed?

Have you set goals for your staff? Are you having weekly, one-on-one meetings with each of your staff members to set (and review) goals that will enable them to increase their pay checks, and thereby in return, increase the salon's overall revenue?

I am a firm believer in setting up goals and incentives for your stylists so that they have a plan going forward.

You may want to start the meeting with your stylist by having her make a dream list of the things she wants to buy in the future when she begins making more money.

Another positive approach to take with your stylist is to break down the dollar goals into something such as "all you have to do is sell x number of products a day to reach your weekly dollar goal," and so on.

Each week, you will need to go over what direction you and your stylist's pre-established goals are headed and then take whatever action you need to turn it in the right direction. Before each one-on-one weekly meeting, make sure you have one to two items planned out that you want to focus on with each stylist. Make sure you have reviewed each stylist's numbers prior to the meeting.

Make sure your goals for your salon coincide with your stylist's goals. Always have a plan that will involve praising and recognizing each stylist to keep the meeting positive. During the meeting, for example, let's say you had set a previous goal with Stylist #1 that she would introduce three new clients to a color service, but at the end of the week she had accomplished only one. You should first ask yourself was the stylist part of setting this goal or was it the owner or manager who set this goal?

Always let the stylist tell you what she thinks she can attain. It is very important that the stylist be accountable for her own goals. It also increases the chance that the goal will be met, since it was not forced on the stylist, and she believes the goal could be attainable. Once she has set her goals with the owner or manager, the one-on-one meetings will involve the owner or manager coaching the stylist on how to meet her goals. For example, create promotions such as 10% off color services for all new clients. This will allow the stylist to have a tool with which to start the conversation about up-selling services with the client. This type of goal setting and follow-up teaches the stylist how to be in control of giving herself a pay raise.

Use a worksheet when you have your stylist one-on-one meetings; it ensures you clarify and document what your stylist has been achieving and the new goals that are being set. I have included an example of a "One-on-One Meeting Worksheet" that you may want to use.

ONE -ON- ONE MEETING WORKSHEET

Name of Stylist:

Manager/Owner:

Date:

SERVICES	PRICE	TOTAL # DONE	TOTAL $ MADE	NEW GOAL #	FORECASTED $ INCREASE	SALON GOAL
Women's Haircut and Finish						
Color Services						
Highlight Services						
Highlight - Lowlight						
Glossing						
5-7 Foils						
Blow Dries						
Kid's Cuts						
Men's Cuts						
Texturizing (Perming)						
Straightening						
Accessorizing The Hair						
Deep Protein Treatments						
Deep Moisturizing Treatments						
Waxing						
Facials						
Teeth Whitening						

During your meeting with your stylist, you may also find it helpful to use this next piece titled "Who Are You?" to help your stylist identify which type of person she would rather be. My stylists always found it very informative to see the bottom line $ figures in black and white!

WHO ARE YOU?

Negative Nellie works a total of 30 hours per week and serves five clients a day, five days a week. She is always bored and gives her clients minimal customer service. She never has goals or a plan of action to grow her business. She gossips and creates drama in the salon. People don' t like being around her negativity. She never hands out her business cards when out in the community. It is just a job for Nellie, not a career. She hardly ever gets requests, even though she has been there over six months.

5 clients a day at $20 per haircut = $100 per day service sales

$100 per day x 5 days per week = $500 gross service sales per week

If the salon is paying Nellie 45% commission on her gross service sales, then:

45% x $500 = $225 (this is Nellie' s gross weekly pay from service sales)

She never sells products, so she earns $0 in product commission sales

$225 (gross service sales pay) + $0 (product commission sales) = **$225 gross pay per week**

Fabulous Fran also works 30 hours per week and also serves fi e clients a day, fi e days a week. She arrives at work dressed well, with make-up on and hair fashionably arranged. Fran values her job and calls it a career. She always treats her clients with care.

Fran believes one can never pamper enough. She wants her clients to always look and feel their best. Fran always has new ideas, hairstyles, color, highlights and cuts for her clients. She takes pride in her work and always goes the extra mile to ensure her client has a fabulous experience. She talks to her clients about products that would help their hair to perform at its best. She always offers a *solution,* not a *product,* for hair needs (I explain this concept in the chapter *Retailing in Action*). Fran is always positive and a team player.

Fran upsells each $20 hair cut into an additional $70 color service (haircut + upsell = $90) so:

5 clients a day x $90 service = $450 per day service sales

$450 per day x 5 days per week = $2,250 gross service sales per week

If the salon is paying Fran 45% commission on her gross service sales, then:

45% x $2,250 = $1,012.50 (this is Fran's gross weekly pay from service sales)

Fran sets a goal of selling five, $15 products per day. $15 x 5 per day = $75 per day. $75 per day x 5 days per week = $375 product sales per week

If the salon is paying Fran 10% commission on her product sales, then:

10% x $375 = $37.50 (this is Fran's weekly product commission pay)

$1,012.50 (gross service sales pay) + $37.50 (product commission sales) =

$1,050 gross pay per week

And by all means, don't forget to make your salon a fun atmosphere for your staff! They are more likely to do well and be loyal to you if they enjoy their working environment.

For example, have theme days in your salon where everyone dresses up as their favorite celebrity. It adds a fun environment, and the stylists will love it. Let them be a part of the voting process as to what themes they would like. This encourages staff participation and support as well.

When you and your staff enjoy being at your salon, your clients will enjoy it too. One of the things I did to create a fun atmosphere was to get a popcorn machine - one of the old fashioned ones for $200.00 - and I offered popcorn on Saturdays and a free picture of children after their haircut.

As I have said before, the ideas are endless. In upcoming chapters, I discuss creating the "aha moment," and I offer many more exciting ideas to keep clients interested and always wondering what you will be doing next.

It is so important for the owner to know how to manage his or her time wisely in order to ensure the best outcome. If you are fi time management to be a problem for you, create a goal and action plan to improve it! Make sure your staff is properly trained and offering the best customer service possible. I sometimes hired a mystery shopper to come into my salon and document everything she witnessed (many companies out there offer this service). I then sat down with my staff, both individually and as a group, to go over the positive statements and how we were to improve on the weak areas.

I am a fi m believer that everything we set out to do starts with a dream; we turn the dream into goals, and then build a business plan based on our goals. Remember, **goals must always be written, attainable, and easy to track.** Taking control back is one of the most empowering actions you can do for your business. I have always said the antidote to fear is knowledge. This book is designed to do just that: give you back control and put you back in charge.

Remember you have to know where you are at currently and then where you want to go. Written goals will help you stay focused. Don' t overwhelm yourself. Have fun!

In the next section, we will be learning the art of advertising on a shoestring budget. I will show you creative ways to get new clients in your door without spending a lot. I will give you lists of ideas, some old and some new, for creating new promotions. I will also offer ideas on how to keep your current clients from going to your competition. My hope is that all this information will get your own creative juices flowing as well, as you create new plans to grow your business.

THE ABC'S OF OPERATING YOUR SALON

SECTION THREE

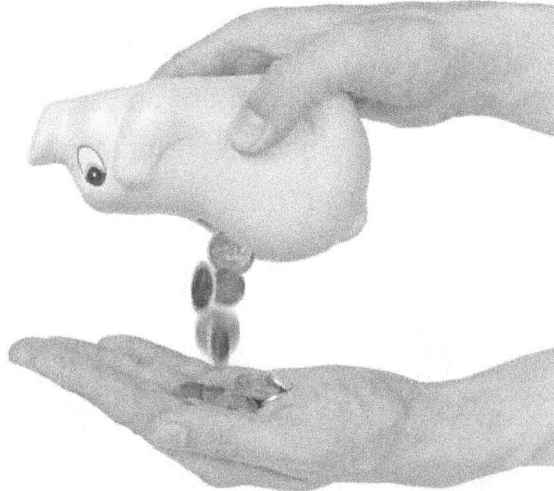

ADVERTISING ON A SHOESTRING BUDGET

In this section, we will be discussing the art of advertising on a shoestring budget. Advertising: a subject that causes many people to sigh! It seems overwhelming, but it doesn' t have to be.

We will learn why a Point of Sale system is so important for your salon.

We will discuss some incentive programs that can help your business grow.

We want to ensure that you are using your money wisely to create the most revenue and, thereby, increase the value of your salon.

I can't tell you how many salons owners and managers I have talked to who don't have any idea what advertising plan is working best and what is bringing back customers. They don't know where they are wasting money.

Let's work to bring the advertising of your salon from an expense to an investment.

You need to measure and track the success of each component of the advertising that you do. This is where a POS (or point of sale) system can be very helpful. It allows you to track all the promotions and/or coupons you have sent out and then tracks them when they come back in. You are able to track which ones bring in new customers and you can even see which are bringing lost clients back in again. This knowledge allows you to focus your time on what works and not waste your time (and money) on what doesn't.

There are many companies that offer POS systems. You can find these companies on the internet. However, I highly recommend that you research POS systems that are geared for salon use.

There are also marketing companies that you can hire to go into your POS system and do mailings at a very affordable price to areas in the select zip codes of your choice. At your request, such marketing companies can also go into your POS system and send gift certificates to all your women who get haircuts only, offering money off when they try a color service with you.

Through your POS system, these marketing companies can also find clients that have not been back for three, six, or nine months and send them a "we miss you letter" with a $5.00 off certificate to entice them back in. They also offer e-mail clubs where they can do extensive e-mail blasts to potential clients and to new clients. The list is endless with companies like this once you have a POS system.

The POS system will give you an end-of-the-day report every evening after you close your salon with all the services your staff did that day separated out into different categories.

A POS system keeps track of what your retention rate is (in other words, how many of your customers keep coming back); it keeps track for your salon as a whole, and it will also keep track of each stylist's record of retention as well. This will allow you to see which of your stylists are bringing back clients and which ones are not. You can then meet with that stylist and reevaluate why she is not bringing back the clients she has previously done.

The POS system will keep records of any redo's that may have happened during the month. It also gives you weekly and monthly reports to view at your convenience.

If you don't already have some form of POS system, I highly recommend you investigate a system that would suit your needs.

Okay, so now that we've covered the importance of being able to track the effectiveness of your advertising, let's look at cost-effective ways to advertise.

Do you find your salon is successful in bringing in new customers? Are you able to bring in clients at a regular rate? Do you have a sufficient number of customers, or are you struggling to get them in the door? And, of course, once you do get customers in the door, are you able to keep them coming back?

Take a moment to jot down your answers to these questions.

Building a successful client base does not have to be complicated. It takes a lot of hard work and preparation, but when it comes to getting new clients, you don't have to spend all of your resources in hopes of getting the return you want.

One of the most cost-effective ways to build your clientele is to rely on your best customers to bring in more customers. This requires that you develop a plan and make sure you continue to see it to fruition. Let's just think for a moment. Which new customer do you think is more valuable, one who finds your business by chance or one who finds your business because a friend told her about it?

In general, referred customers are more valuable because they already have a level of trust with your stylists and salon, and, also importantly, it cost little or nothing to get them in the door. Therefore, from the minute that customer walks through the door, each sale you make to her is more profitable for you.

So how do you develop a referral system that works for your business?

Start by providing the best possible service for your existing customers, especially those customers that come in on a regular basis. How to provide the best customer service is a topic we go into in more depth further on in this book.

Next, review your incentive programs. Do you have a good incentive program set up for your top customers? For example, when these customers tell their friends and family about you, they should receive something from you such as a discounted product or service. If your clients love your business, they MAY tell other people about you, but if they love YOU, and you make it worth their while, they WILL tell other people about you.

One popular incentive program that I have seen many salons use with great success is the referral business card program. The cards are intended for stylists to hand out to each client after their service. That card should have a space for your client to fill in her name and address. The referral card offers the potential new client an incentive to come in, such as 50% off your first visit. Make the offer as intriguing and as enticing as possible.

Each time a new client brings in the card with your current client' s name, you will mail your current client something as a thank you. I used to mail them a $5.00 gift certificate to be used at their next service. Everyone wins with this promotion: the new client, the current client, and the salon. This starts to build a strong client base with very little expense to you.

Every time a client goes out of their way to send us a friend or family member it is a tremendous opportunity for us to grow our business, not to mention the positive message our loyal client is giving by sending us a referral. But what is one loyal customer sending us referrals on a regular basis really worth? Use the following equation to see.

Follow steps 1-5, plugging in your own numbers. (See the example below.)

1. Value of each guest (your current average ticket)

2. Guest refers three people (current average ticket x 3)

3. Each guest visits eight times a year (line 2 x 8)

4. Number of years as guest (average is 5 years) (line 3 x 5-year average)

5. What are they worth?

For Example:

1. Value of each client (your current average ticket) = **$40.00**

2. Your client refers three people: **3 X $40.00 = $120.00**

3. Each client visits eight times a year: **$120.00 X 8 = $960.00**

4. Number of years as a client (average is 5 years): **$960.00 X 5 = $4,800.00 That is the worth of a referral.**

As you can see, you should never underestimate the value of referrals! So, keeping in mind that your cost for bringing in referred clients is little to nothing, you can see why one of the best forms of advertising is word of mouth. Let your clients do the work and you focus on the best customer service possible. Again, in the next chapters, I show you how to give the client the best possible experience ever, making her want to tell the world about your salon.

Remember, statistics show that 80% of the reason a client returns to your salon is because of the experience they had while being serviced at your salon. The other 20%

of customers say they return because of the actual service done. A client who is happy with your salon and services is more likely to forgive an occasional haircut that it not of the same quality that they are accustomed to (because we all have our bad days), but they will look elsewhere if they have received poor customer service.

Another great way of advertising with little or no expense is to involve your salon in the community.

Become a sponsor for your local youth sports teams, for example, the little league team.

Hold cut-a-thons for your favorite charity. A lot of newspapers and radio stations will advertise for free when it is done for charities. For example, when I owned my salon, I would support breast cancer awareness week. I would write a letter to the breast cancer association and let them know that I was supporting their charity for a specific week or month with a portion of the salon's proceeds going to the charity. In return, they would send me a letter to verify the event. I would submit the letter to all local advertising venues, and my salon would receive advertising from radio stations on the hour or in print in the local paper.

Don't overlook networking with other companies in your area. For example, network with Weight Watchers and/or Curves, offering their clients 10% off their first visit - or every visit; it can be whatever you choose.

Try linking up with a local boutique to do hair and makeup for their next fashion show.

Offer military and other service people a VIP business card to keep in their wallet to use when getting their haircut, offering them a discount, such as 15% off their haircuts.

Make up special packages for nurses and medical staff at the hospitals near you. I was very successful in doing this in my salons.

Make out VIP cards for students, then hand them out to all your teenage clients to give to their friends.

You can also visit schools and offer a free demonstration on extensions, hairstyling, etc. This can be particularly lucrative before prom time.

The following handout, "Marketing Business Tools," offers more detail on some of the advertising and marketing suggestions I just discussed, and there are more suggestions as well that you may find useful.

MARKETING BUSINESS TOOLS

VIP CARD

- Customize the card with your particular salon information as well as the specific discount that you want to provide.

- Use these cards as local business discount cards within a nearby shopping center.

- VIP cards can also be used for military, police, firemen, and nurses.

SENIOR DISCOUNT FLYER

- Distribute or post a flyer in your salon to promote senior business hours.

- Use the days or hours in your salon that are slowest to promote this event. (Mornings and early afternoons usually work best – but avoid weekends, as these are your busiest days). The idea is to build business at a time when you normally have a lull in services.

- If you are interested in distributing this flyer, check with local senior community centers or churches.

COLOR EXTRAVAGANZA FLYER

- Pass them out locally.

- Provide one to all clients who visit your salon.

- The idea is to plan an event that promotes color services to your clients who normally do not have them done.

- Make it a fun event with your staff.

• Promote an event like this weeks in advance to build momentum and interest.

SALON NEWSLETTER

• Great tool for promoting services and retail to your existing clients.

• Create a monthly or bi-monthly newsletter to inform clients of retail promotions, service specials and salon events.

• Feature a specific product each issue or even talk about your staff.

• Take the opportunity to promote all you offer in your salon.

• You can create them and print them, or you can distribute them electronically, which will cost you nothing.

OTHER MARKETING OPPORTUNITIES

• Check with the Parent-Teacher groups at your local schools.

   ✓ Student organizations (student governments, pep teams, orchestra and band) are always looking to build funds and retain sponsors for events.

   ✓ Schools have athletic departments that offer great promotion opportunities – sponsor/host the sports teams and cheerleading league.

   ✓ Student papers are always looking for businesses to post ads in their publications. (At prom time, place an ad about up-dos. For spring, feature a coupon for highlighting services. Offer an honor roll discount, rewarding students with great grades. Get creative, because the possibilities are endless. Don't underestimate the power of using a school paper—they offer you great exposure to teens).

• The same goes for college newspapers and university publications.

   ✓ Once again, you have a direct link to a target audience.

✓ Offer a discount when students present their college ID card in your salon.

✓ If the college has a radio station, you can purchase on-air promotions or ads for a great price.

✓ See if there is a dormitory council. Each semester, new students move into the dorms – usually these students are given information packets that include coupons for local businesses in the direct vicinity of the college.

- Contact owners and managers of apartments and rentals. Ask to put your salon's information in the welcome packet new renters receive upon moving in.

- Community publications are great for your business for two reasons.

  ✓ The smaller the publication, the more inexpensive it is to place an ad.

  ✓ They focus on targeting an audience in a concentrated area. In a small community paper, you'll have more of a chance of being noticed.

- Cross-promote with local businesses in your area.

  ✓ Tanning salons

  ✓ Nail salons

  ✓ Bridal boutiques

  ✓ Fitness centers, etc.

  ✓ Many of these businesses are looking to cross-promote with you as well.

  ✓ Knock on some doors and see what opportunities are available to you. Just keep in mind that the business next door is not always your competition – chances are you share some of the same potential clients.

- Churches host a variety of events throughout the year.

  ✓ Check to see if they publish their events in a paper or newsletter to their members. You may be surprised how many parishes in your neighborhood are willing to take advantage of any assistance or promotions you can offer.

There are so many cost-effective ways to market your business. The ideas are endless! Be creative and make it fun.

Another hidden secret I want to be sure you are aware of is a wonderful incentive program, which because I found it to be so successful in my salons, I offer it directly on my website. This program utilizes vacation certificates as an incentive to encourage clients to spend more in your salon. I also used them as performance incentives for my staff.

Vacation certificates are not associated in any way with time-share properties. The certificates work so well because the cost is minimal for you to purchase, yet they have a high-perceived value to your customers and staff. The way it works is the salon owner buys the certificates for only $4-5 per certificate, depending on the volume purchased. Each certificate is for a three day, two night hotel stay and is valued up to $180, depending on the geographical location and hotel selection.

You can utilize these certificates to provide your customers, and staff, with a meaningful reward that they can actually use.

You will find that when you give out these vacation certificates:

✓ You will increase your sales by motivating your team to out-perform.

✓ You will retain your top performers.

✓ You will create repeat business: existing clients will have an incentive to return more frequently and to spend more money each time.

✓ You will attract new clients and generate referrals.

✓ You will outperform your competition and create a unique position in the marketplace.

✓ Give your customers more than they expect by increasing the value of the service you provide to them, and they will love you and your business for it.

On my website, www.PositiveSalonStrategies.com, click on "Vacation Certificates" for more information and great ideas on how to use the incentive certificates.

Remember, knowing what advertising plans, referral plans, and incentive programs are working best for you is very important. You do not want to waste your resources on programs that are not providing a good return for your salon. Your time and money are valuable, and you want to make them count for all they are worth!

On the next pages you will find three "handouts" I have used over the years to give you even more promotional ideas; take from them any suggestions that sound good to you, and of course, add your own ideas too!

The Fabulous Forty

Stumped for fresh ideas when it comes to creating new promotions? Here's a starter set of 40 ideas. Some are old, some are new, some may appeal to you and some may not. Use this material as food for thought to get your own creative juices flowing.

1. Hold a cut-a-thon for charity.

2. Link up with a local boutique to do hair and makeup for their next fashion show.

3. Sponsor a Little League or Walk-A-Thon team.

4. Suggest a free home care assembly program at local high schools.

5. Make news and send out press releases covering it.

6. Hold a seasonal hair fashion show with refreshments.

7. Write a letter to the editor and sign it with your own name and the name of your salon.

8. Donate a hair styling or perm for a local charity auction.

9. Put your salon's menu up on college and church bulletin boards.

10. Buy several small display ads in the newspaper instead of one larger ad.

11. Advertise in the classifieds.

12. Do a bulk mailing introducing your salon and its services to non-clients in your area.

13. Offer one of your local female newscasters – or all of them – a cosmetic make-over, then get a photographer to take pics and mail out the press release.

14. Suggest yourself as a radio talk show guest to discuss the latest salon techniques.

15. Hold a series of weekly in-salon seminars on makeup and hair care.

16. Request information about co-op advertising from manufacturers whose products you retail.

17. Hold a senior citizen's special.

18. Order salon t-shirts and offer them at a discounted price to your clients or use them as crossover marketing.

19. Pass out brochures at your local shopping mall.

20. Advertise in the yellow pages.

21. Run a sweepstakes, perhaps with a salon gift certificate as a prize.

22. Offer a "TRY ME" special on your least requested secondary service.

23. Give a limited time "BRING A FRIEND" discount.

24. Offer reasonably priced catered lunches or sandwiches over the noon hour for the working woman.

25. Have a "CHILDREN'S DAY" haircut program.

26. Give brochures listing all your services to existing clients.

27. Cross-market retail items. Use a pretty ribbon to tie a vented brush around a bottle of shampoo.

28. Hold a mousse and gel "clinic" to demonstrate spiking and scrunching methods.

29. Invite your newspaper's lifestyles editor to lunch and a tour of the salon.

30. Start a salon newsletter.

31. Network with professionals in other businesses through your chamber of commerce.

32. Check with other local small businesses about swapping mailing lists.

33. Start sending birthday cards to clients.

34. Spotlight a different retail item every week.

35. Think of a creative promotion for every holiday. Sound impossible? It's not.

36. Start changing your displays and smaller items of décor on a regular basis.

37. Promote your most positive points by offering a gift if you fail to live up to them. "We pride ourselves on our scheduling···we promise you $5 off every 15 minutes of waiting time."

38. Motivate your staff with a reward for increased business.

39. Hold an anniversary party. Send out press releases to community news editors.

40. Read the "business ledger" section of the newspaper and send $10 gift certificates with letters of congratulations to people whose promotions are announced.

Seventeen Ways to Win the Working Woman

Have you "stretched" enough to reach the working woman? Or have you thought of her as "just another salon client" and made no attempt to offer her something your competition hasn't considered? Here are seventeen promotional ideas for winning over the working woman. We hope you've tried some of them already. Why not make a point of checking off the ones that might be right for your salon? Then prioritize the ideas you've checked and make plans to put them into action. Always remember that success is something that you make happen!

1. **Offer lunch or snacks** – this doesn't have to be a complicated operation. If you're near a coffee shop, perhaps you can make arrangements for delivery. Or you could give clients the option of a pre-ordered box lunch and pack the lunches yourself. Many women can't afford the time to visit the salon and fit in lunch too.

2. **Offer a simultaneous service package** – promote a "working woman's special," promising to deliver a cut, blow dry and manicure all in just an hour appointment. Then coordinate the manicurist's schedule so she'll be working on the client's nails during the styling.

3. **Set up wireless internet for your business clients** – so they can work while they wait for their appointment or while they are getting a time-consuming service.

4. **Suggest a demonstration for your local woman's business group** – a talk on "dressing for success" or "office grooming" will usually be welcome.

5. **Consider changing your hours** – many salons are reaching the working woman by opening earlier, closing later and/or adding Sunday hours.

6. **Network with a clothing store for a shopper's special** – this is a good promotion for Thursday evenings when shops have late hours. You could offer clients a 15% discount, good for only that same night, at a local shop, asking the shop to do the same for you.

7. **Set special business women's hours during which there will be an image consultant at no charge** – not only will you be offering working women a benefit, the image consultant can sell perms and color for you.

8. Link up with a secretarial service or free-lance secretary – you can offer this service – if booked in advance – for women who want to catch up on correspondence or other work while they're in the salon.

9. **Promote pedicures** – a discounted pedicure is hard for women to resist – especially for those whose jobs call for a lot of time spent standing.

10. **Fill your reception area with a lot of mail order catalogues** – then get the word out that clients can shop by mail in the salon. You could even photocopy extra order forms for their convenience. If you have free internet service (as was mentioned earlier), your clients can order from their laptops or mobile devices.

11. **Develop a tie-in with a local spa or health club** – today's working woman is often health and figure conscious.

12. **Give an "on-time" guarantee** – women with jobs are on tight schedules. Promise a big percentage off the total service bill if a client's waiting time is more than so many minutes. This is a good gimmick, as it proclaims your faith in the smooth running of your salon.

13. **Hold a stress seminar** – you may want to barter with an expert to demonstrate stress-relief techniques in the salon.

14. **Do a mailing to large companies for Secretary's Day** – write directly to the company's president, offering specials for Secretary's Day gifts. You might offer

$20 gift certificates with increasing discounts (i.e., boss pays $18 each for 3-5, $15 each for 5-10, $14 each for more than 10).

15. **Arrange for babysitting service** – setting an area aside for tots (and having a sitter present) will attract working mothers.

16. **Hold a drawing for a computer or microwave** – both of these items are coveted by most businesswomen.

17. **Offer a wine and cheese after hours special** – what a nice way to end the day, especially when her special service is accompanied by a relaxing scalp and neck massage.

Male Call
Promotional ideas to bring men into your salon

1. **Team Power** – get the press involved with free "hair makeovers" for top players on any sports teams that have high visibility.

2. **Celebrity Clout** – barter salon services with local anchormen or disc jockeys in return for endorsements.

3. **Father and Son Day** – give dads a half-price haircut if they bring in their son for a haircut at the same time.

4. **Boss's Day** – print up special gift certificates for bosses and sell them for a gift.

5. **Members Only** – set aside a day when specific club members (Elks, Rotary, etc.) receive discounts.

6. **For Men Only** – schedule a men's seminar with advice and information on men's services and hairpieces.

7. **King for a Day** – offer "the works" (cut, beard or mustache trim, facial, manicure) at a special package price.

8. **Men's Night** – set aside time one evening a week that is for men only.

9. **Gift for the Groom** – give "the works" free to the groom who brings in all of his ushers and best man.

10. Two for One – two for one special for any man who comes in with a (male) pal.

THE ABC'S OF OPERATING YOUR SALON

SECTION FOUR

HIRING AND RETAINING LOYAL STAFF

One of the most frequently asked questions I get from salon owners is: "How do I get my staff to work hard, be loyal to my salon, and not leave, taking their clientele with them?" Most salon owners put a great deal of time and money into training staff. What I hear all too often is that the work ethic of some people in this current, younger generation is not acceptable. I hear frequent complaints that this generation has a lack of understanding that it takes hard work to build a client base because there is a certain "sense of entitlement" that things will be handed to them on a silver platter. In addition, there is an expectation that a lot of money will be made quickly. When I owned my salons, it always baffled me that my staff thought I was a millionaire and should offer them the moon. Wow! As salon owners, we know so differently.

In my own salons, I decided to put a plan into action that helped me out immensely. It did not, 100 percent, take away this problem of turnover and lack of loyalty, but it reduced it by at least 70 percent.

The plan starts right from the interviewing process. As the owner, you need to have an organized plan of action when choosing the right candidate for your salon. Here are some points to take into consideration.

First and foremost, create an employee handbook with all the rules of the salon, your expectations, and a consequence list for prospective staff to read and understand and then sign when they are hired. Your handbook should explain in detail a list of unacceptable actions that are against salon policy and the expectant consequences of those particular actions. The consequence may be one verbal warning, a written warning, or grounds for immediate termination. You need to be clear about what the exact repercussion will be; for example, if a staff member receives three verbal warnings, a written warning follows with a probation period. If the action continues, termination will follow. If you believe that certain unacceptable behaviors should result in immediate termination with no prior warning (such as theft), that needs to be clearly stated. Keep a very detailed file on each employee in case you will ever need it down the road for verifying information, for unemployment, lawsuits, etc. Having a clear list of unacceptable behaviors and subsequent consequences leaves nothing to be misunderstood if the inappropriate behavior occurs.

I found that having such a handbook helped my staff to feel I was being fair with each of them, and not "playing favorites." This was especially helpful in the more gray areas of my expectations. For example in my salons I would not tolerate gossip or back stabbing, and there was no room for prima donnas. I would give a warning for this behavior, and my staff quickly realized that no one was exempt from this expectation.

In addition to an employee handbook ensuring that my staff and I had a clear understanding of the salon policies, it also provided written material for me to refer back to with my staff, showing them that they signed it, indicating they understood the policies and had agreed to follow them. It also minimized staff members trying to use the excuse that they did not know that a certain policy or expectation existed.

The following information is a handout I would give to members of my salon management team to provide them with guidelines of what my expectations were. I believed it was very important for a staff to understand the reasons for having an employee handbook and to ensure that we were all on the same page.

THE IMPORTANCE OF AN EMPLOYEE HANDBOOK

- If your team does not know the "rules," then they cannot be held responsible when they don' t measure up to your expectations.

- Team member handbooks must include all the salon' s policies and procedures.

- Each team member should receive a copy of the handbook and sign a receipt stating that they have read and understand the content of the handbook.

- If employees know the rules and vision of the salon, then they will feel confident to make decisions.

- An employee handbook is a communication tool designed to empower employers, managers and employees with a consistent approach to accomplishing their daily tasks.

- It provides a set of policies, procedures, forms and work routines that convey the pulse of the organization.

- A properly developed manual focuses everyday business communications between employees and managers on what is really important to get the job done.

- This handbook is the first step in the implementation process of communicating the policies and procedures within a salon.

- Use an employee manual as a starting point.

- Create an easy to read policy guide with descriptions as a reference for employees.

- Hold staff meetings to give guidance, direction and training for policies or procedures.

- Create huddles so all employees have a voice in the implementation process.

- Have coaching sessions for employees who require more involvement in the implementation process.

- Create a reward system to assist in the support of the implementation process.

- A key aspect of a reward system is to recognize compliance efforts so that employees perceive that it is in their best interest to support policies and procedures.

- Rewards do not need to be costly or time consuming.

- Involve team members so they "buy in."

- Award suggestions:

➢ Best Attendance Award

➢ Best Dressed Award

➢ Employee of the Month Award

Ø Best Customer Service Award

Ø Early Bird Award

➢ Best Team Player

➢ Best Award for Up-selling

➢ Best Award for Retailing

Because I believe so strongly in putting things in writing, I used a "discipline sheet" as a guide in my salons. I am including it here so that you may use it as a reference when you are creating your own written policies and procedures. I used to put the form on the wall in the lunch room so everyone could view it whenever they wanted to. I could then answer any questions my stylists might have.

DISCIPLINE SHEET

The Written Warning

- A written warning serves as a formal notice that a serious infraction has occurred.

- Written warnings should state the nature of the offense, method of correction, and action to be taken if offense is repeated.

- A written warning also serves to gain the employee' s agreement that this will be the last time that a problem needs to be addressed.

The Verbal Warning

- Example:

"As you were informed prior to your employment here, this salon has a career apparel of black and white clothing, which you are not dressed in. I will provide you with a black smock to wear today during your shift, however, starting tomorrow I'll expect that you will be in proper salon attire."

The Final Warning

- Its purpose is to inform the employee that his/her job is in jeopardy of being lost.

- Example of a final warning:

"You were scheduled to work this Saturday. When you did not appear at the salon, the manager called you to find out if you had planned on reporting to work that day. You stated that you would be in within the hour. You failed to show or call the salon. If this situation repeats

itself, it will be considered job abandonment and you will be termi-
nated from this salon."

Reasons for Warnings

- The employee does not meet performance criteria

- The employee has violated your policies and procedures

- The employee is in constant conflict with you or others they work with

- The employee consistently has personal problems that are interfering with his/her job performance

Before Giving a Warning, Ask Yourself These Questions

- Does the employee understand his/her job responsibilities?

- Does the employee understand the consequences of negative behavior?

- Did the employee understand and sign the salon policy handbook?

During the Warning Process

- Make sure you have proof of poor performance

- Does the employee's explanation have merit?

- Have you done everything to give the employee the benefit of the doubt?

Types of Discipline

- Consequence chart

- Coaching sessions

- Counseling sessions

- Verbal reminders

- Increase "check-ups" on job performance

- Oral reprimand (verbal warning)

- Written reprimand (written warning)

- Temporarily sending them home

- Reducing hours

- Temporary probation

- Termination

For example, after 3 verbal warnings and 2 written warnings, then the last step before termination is suspension

- The purpose of the suspension is to let the team member know the seriousness of the problem

- The suspension should be used as a "cooling off " period in which to resolve the problem if possible

When to Terminate

- Possessing, being under the influence of, or using alcoholic beverages or drugs

- Possessing dangerous weapons

- Immoral or indecent conduct, soliciting persons for immoral purposes, or the aiding or abetting any of the above

- Theft or misappropriation of guest's, team member's, or company property, or unauthorized removal of any of the above

- Fighting or provoking a fight with a guest or a team member

- Abusing or destroying company property, the property of guests, or the property of other team members

- Taking or "borrowing" cash

- Falsifying company documents

BEFORE DISCIPLINING

Consider:

- Does the team member's explanation raise any circumstances or compelling sympathies?

- Should there be an action less than discipline? (i.e., coaching)

- Does all management agree with the discipline decision?

- Can you show proof of poor performance?

- Have you done everything possible to help this person?

Do's and Don'ts When Meeting with a Stylist About Warnings:

DO'S: Be specific about expectations

              Focus on performance

              Make consequences clear

              Be fair and even in your discipline process

DON'Ts: Be vague

              Focus on personalities

              Play favorites

As I have mentioned, you must keep accurate written documentation in your employee records. The following is an example of an Employee Warning Report for you to use and adapt as necessary for your specific needs.

Employee Warning Report (EXAMPLE)

Employee's Name:_

Violation Date:_   Violation Time:_

Description of violation: _

_____

- _ **First Verbal Warning**. Date given:_

- _ **First Written Warning**; verbal warning was given (date:) and has not corrected situation. Date of written warning:_

- _ **First Written Warning, verbal warning has not been given.** Situation is serious enough to warrant immediate written warning. Date:_

- _ **Final Written Warning** (give dates of previous warnings)

Date of this warning:_

First verbal:_   First written:_

Any additional warnings and dates:_

- _ **Suspension.** Date:_

Indicate the behavior contributing to this warning:

- _ Attendance   - _ Unprepared for work

- _ Disobedience   - _ Appearance (not up to salon

- _ Tardiness   standards). Describe:_

- _ Safety   _____

- _ Work quality   - _ Other (specify):_

- _ Gossip

_____

Consequence Chart

In this section, write examples of consequences for your salon:

What will constitute a verbal warning

What will constitute a written warning (i.e., 1 prior verbal warning for the same or similar offense)

What will constitute probation or reduction of hours (i.e., 3 verbal warnings & 1 written warning)

What will constitute immediate termination (i.e., 1 warning after probation)

So, along with your written employee handbook and your clearly documented position on discipline, each position in your salon (such as manager, salon coordinator, front desk staff, and stylist) must have its own written job description. Again, this presents to staff members exactly what is expected of them in their specific position. If you don't already have job descriptions written out, here is an example of one for a Salon Manager that you can review.

SALON MANAGER JOB DESCRIPTION

The salon manager(s)' responsibilities include these key tasks:

1. Recruit, hire and schedule salon staff.

- Recruit
- Interview
- Hire
- Set up work schedules

2. Oversee training of salon staff.

- Schedule stylists to class
- Handle new team member orientation
- Consistently coach for better skills

- Train thoroughly in safety issues

3. Evaluate performance of salon staff.

- Evaluate
- Discipline
- Promote
- Terminate

4. Effectively motivate all staff.

- Staff meetings
- Promotions and contests
- Formal and informal recognition

5. Promote excellence in customer service.

- Constant training and emphasis
- Customer relations, tracking, complaints, redo's

6. Control cash functions.

- Daily deposits, inventorying, refunds

7. Manage the image and appearance of the salon.

- Adhere to Quality Assurance standards, both for stylist appearance and salon appearance

8. Build the growth and profit of the salon.

- Promotions
- Attend technical classes (one per month or whenever available in your region)
- Attend manager classes – regional and national

———————————————

At this point you should have written down how you want things to be done and what you expect of each potential employee before they even start.

THE KEY, before they start. By providing written expectations, you can better gauge applicants by their reaction to these expectations, and you also give applicants a clear understanding of whether your salon is a good fit for them. The more information you can provide up front, the better it will be in the long run.

Let the interview begin. Have all your questions written out before hand and make sure you read the applicant's resume first so you can elaborate and familiarize yourself with their background, skills and experience.

- Open the interview by talking about your salon.

- State exactly what the job is and exactly what you are looking for as far as hours and skills.

- Go over all of the applicant's qualifications, work history, if any, and whether or not this applicant has the basic requirements and type of background for the position you are looking to fill.

- Is the personality of the candidate that of a team player?

- Did he/she come professionally dressed and groomed for the interview?

- Carefully explain what your expectations are for the position, such as dress code, flexible hours, mandatory weekends, etc.

- If you have a set pay scale, share what your compensation package is and discuss their past compensation and what you are offering.

- Explain any retailing expectations you may have for them, including percentages. Be clear about what type of production per hour you are looking for, making sure they fully understand what you are asking of them.

- If you are interested in the candidate, then you can ask for references and permission to check them. Please CALL THEM. It can save you so many headaches in the future.

- Now to close the interview, ask if there are any questions. Tell them whom to call if they have questions. If you know they are a strong candidate, then set up a technical interview next. If you are unsure at this point, state that you have other candidates to interview, and you will call them back in x number of days, either way.

A technical interview is very important, and it is an element that is so often overlooked. It can save you major headaches down the road. Even if the stylist is seasoned, he or she may be weak in certain areas such as chemical services, men's cuts, perms, etc. I recommend you have the applicant bring in a model, and you should also have a mannequin available for them to place foils, perm rods, rollers, etc. It will give you an idea of what additional training, if any, may be necessary to bring the stylist up to expectations.

Something else I would do was let my manager sit in on the interview so we could compare notes after. I often times included my staff as well in meeting the new candidate and then getting their feedback. This made them feel part of the hiring process, and they were more apt to accept and invite the stylist readily because they felt part of the final decision. A team mentality for everyone is a must in order for a salon to do well.

When you hire a stylist, I strongly recommend you offer at least a week of orientation. Walk them through all you want them to know about the salon and how things function. Designate a senior stylist to take the new stylists under his/her wing to become familiar with where everything is. If the new stylist needs some form of education, this is the time to incorporate it. I always positioned my new stylist's styling station next to a senior stylist or my manager. This buddy system is a great way to make the new stylist comfortable and less nervous. When the new stylist is not servicing a client, he/she can observe the technical skills of the mentoring stylist.

Preparation is the key to success in getting the right staff in your salon.

Now let's address how to develop staff loyalty and how to help them want to be the very best they can be once you have hired them. I learned early on that appreciation goes a long way.

I used to have my staff decorate a bag of their choice, and I would hang the bags in the back room. About once a week, either I, or my manager, would write a special note to each stylist that was positive, and expressing appreciation, and place it in her bag. I would have a pizza party just to say "thank you" once a month. I would get $10 gas cards or coffee shop cards to show appreciation for a particular stylist who was doing a great job. Showing appreciation to your staff can be as simple as a kind word, making them feel special. I treated my staff with respect, and I expected that my staff would be respectful to me, and to each other, in return.

Be sure that when a problem arises to nip it in the bud as soon as possible by having a one-on-one meeting with the particular staff member to stop whatever is happening so it won't spread throughout the salon.

It takes time to get a great staff, so it should be a priority for salon owners and managers to KEEP their great staff. It is our job as a salon owner or manager to understand how each individual differs and to learn how to deal with different types of personalities, all whom carry different issues with them into your salon.

I truly believe we, salon professionals, choose this field in the first place because we have open and willing hearts, and we honestly want to make people feel better about themselves. We feel rewarded from doing for others. However, there are times when we allow ourselves to get caught up in everyday problems, negativities, and old destructive thought patterns. Having different personalities all trying to work in sync under the same roof of a salon takes great skill. If you, the salon owner, understand the importance of recognizing that we all have weaknesses, imperfections, and differences and are willing to be patient and proactive in dealing with problems (and don't ignore them, hoping they will go away), you are way ahead of the game. If you can make it a priority to utilize your position as owner or manager to honestly help each individual in your salon achieve personal and business success, all else will fall into place. The rest is fundamental: One-on-one meetings, setting goals, praise, appreciation, and getting to know each person that is working for you on an individual level.

So remember, when it comes to retaining a loyal staff:

Management fails when they fail to provide...

- clarity about expectations

- clarity about career development and earning potential

- regular feedback about performance

- regular scheduled huddles/meetings

- a framework within which the employee perceives they can succeed

- clear communication about expectations to the employee

- frequent feedback and make the employee feel valued

- sharing of their ideas of what contributes to the success of the employee

Managers retain staff when they...

- praise

- pay employees fairly and well

- treat each and every employee with respect

- show them that you care about their accomplishments and attempts

- clearly communicate goals, responsibilities and expectations

- recognize performance appropriately and consistently

- involve employees in plans and decisions, especially those that affect them

- create opportunities for employees to learn and grow

- actively listen to employees' concerns - both work related and personal

- share information promptly, openly and clearly

- celebrate successes and milestones reached

Why stylists say they stay at a certain salon...

- exciting and challenging work

- career growth

- working with great people

- fair pay

- supportive management

- being recognized/valued

- benefits

- making a difference

- pride in the organization

- great work environment

- autonomy/creativity

- flexibility

- job stability

- fun environment

- loyalty of management to staff

This brings us back to the question I asked earlier: Are you working IN your business or ON your business? You need the time to work ON your business in order to be successful, and much of that time is spent dealing with staff. Being a salon owner involves so many different facets, and I certainly hope you have learned some new things to try. I also hope this book will help you get organized, stay focused, and guide you as you grow your salon to become the absolute best it can be!

My Action Plan for Creating a Loyal Staff

What first change will you make in your current practice for hiring and retaining staff?

_____

_____

_____

_____

List the steps you will take to implement this change.

_____

_____

_____

_____

List other changes you will make in your staff hiring and retention practices in the order in which you will implement them.

_____

_____

_____

_____

_____

_____

_____

On separate sheets of paper: If you do not already have a salon policy handbook, list the expectations and rules you would like your staff to follow. Next compose a consequence list. Be sure to clearly state your expectations of all behaviors that you consider to be unacceptable and then clearly connect the consequence, or sequence of consequences, that staff can expect if the specific salon policy is not followed. Type your handbook and copy or print it for all staff.

On separate sheets of paper: If you do not already have written job descriptions for each staff position in your salon, put those descriptions in writing. Be sure each staff member receives a copy.

Take your time when writing your policy handbook and job descriptions so that you can include as much information as possible. The more detailed you are, the easier it will be for you and your staff going forward.

We have covered a tremendous amount of information in this chapter, *The ABC's of Operating Your Salon.* We've discussed finances, goals and incentives, and we have covered how to develop and write action plans. We've looked at time and money wasters, and we've discussed the art of advertising. We have gone over suggestions for hiring, and retaining, a loyal staff.

In the next chapter, *Hush! Royalty is Walking Through the Door!*, we will discuss how you can (and should) stand out from your competition, how to develop promotions that are fun (as well as lucrative) for your salon, and we will detail how to create an image and atmosphere in your salon that will attract and retain loyal customers.

CHAPTER TWO

HUSH! ROYALTY IS WALKING
THROUGH THE DOOR!

HUSH! ROYALTY IS WALKING THROUGH HE DOOR!

SECTION ONE

HOW TO GROW YOUR CUSTOMER BASE

The fact that we are able to compete within the same industry is part of what makes our society great, but learning how to succeed with competition all around you can be quite a challenge.

In this chapter, you will learn how to bring out your best and how to stand out from your competition.

We will talk about how to develop promotions that are fun for your client and lucrative for your salon.

We will discuss the importance of the image you are portraying in your salon and the importance of giving that unexpected customer service.

We will continue to elaborate on something we have touched on before, which is, in order to compete, you must know your competitions' strengths and weaknesses.

For a client, going to the salon serves as so much more than just getting her hair done. It is a chance to relax and unwind, enjoy being pampered, and possibly catch up on all the gossip with a friend. For many clients, visiting a salon for a specific service provides a social experience that cannot be found in other places. Therefore, it is important to realize that the atmosphere in a salon as well the personalities of the salon staff combine together to form the vital ingredients that ultimately separate one salon from another. For this reason, a person's salon choice can be based as much on these attributes as on a stylist's skills.

The very first step you must take when planning to outshine your competition is to know who you are competing with. To accomplish this you will need to research the salons in your area for numerous pieces of information; you want to know what their prices are, what services they provide, and what kind of extras they are offering.

When I owned my salons, I would make it a point to personally visit different salons in my area to see how my salon could be better and how we could outperform them in all areas.

For a quick example, at one time, we had several local salons that offered drastically low prices, such as a $4.99 haircut. I used to advertise that we took pride in our work and our ability to fix $4.99 haircuts!

I do suggest that it is better to compete in services rather than trying to compete in price. For example, if none of the salons in your area are offering hair extensions as a service you need to jump on the bandwagon, get your staff trained, and start advertising.

Once you define the areas where you see your salon could excel and become unique, you should create a written plan outlining how you will elaborate your services and advertise your niche. Since we covered writing goals and action plans in Chapter One, *The ABC's of Operating Your Salon*, I hope you have a good idea of to how to do this now. If you still feel unclear, please review the first chapter because creating a written plan is one of the keys to your success.

If you don't want to compete with your competition on price (and I think it's a good idea not to) then focus on areas in which you can excel. For example, I used to take pride in how my salon catered to children. We offered snacks, hot chocolate, sodas and ice pops in the summer. I advertised a play area, and on weekends we had free babysitting while parents got their hair done. It was amazing how we grew our kids business and in turn won the business of the fathers and then the mothers.

During the time a parent is bringing in their children, you can present all the services you offer to the parents. Always be on the lookout for situations such as these that offer amazing growth potential. In this particular salon of mine, I found that once we won over the child, then the father would try us out and then the mother. Each time a parent brings their child in to your salon, be sure to give the parent a gift certificate of some kind to try out one of your services.

Let me point out something that is very important to all salons. If you have ten salons in a three-mile radius of your salon, and each salon has ten stylists, that is 100 reasons why a client does not have to come to you. They have 100 other stylists in your area to try to see where they will receive the best customer service.

So, you must offer the client the unexpected visit. A client expects a salon to be clean, with courteous and friendly staff, good service, and so on. And the client may be able to find all of this at numerous different salons in your area. Therefore, you need to give them something that will surprise them and result in the "aha" unforgettable experience.

It all begins with the first impression. The first impression is most important, and it is made by the client in the first three seconds of entering the salon. Unfortunately, in the beauty business, we are judged by the book cover since we are dealing with the public on such an intimate level.

Therefore, first, it is crucial to make sure that your salon and each member of your staff is expressing a professional image. Your salon should be sparkling clean, and your products should be neatly displayed.

All of your staff should be well-groomed, hair styled to a T, makeup on, and wearing nice, professional clothing. Image is everything in our industry.

We support the beauty industry, and we sell beauty to our clients. Therefore, each stylist, herself, must look impeccable and remember that she is advertising hairstyles and hair color on a daily basis. So you need to make sure that your stylists are walking advertisements for your salon! If the stylist is wearing a new, trendy, hairstyle, the client may want the very same color and style. Your stylists should change their hairstyles on a continual basis. You cannot expect your clients to change their look into more exciting, updated styles if your staff members never change their hair.

Please be sure your staffs' hairstyles and colors are suitable to what you can offer your clients and also reflect the clients you are looking to attract. For example, a stylist who wears a conservative style will usually attract conservative clients. The more progressive the stylist' s hair, the more progressive the clients she will likely attract.

Over the years, I have become a true believer that stylists must always use the salon products that are for sale. I have found if the stylist does not like a product, she will not sell it.

If she loves the product, it will fly off the shelf.

So now that we have explored the importance of the image your salon portrays, next, we need to look at your front desk. Who you have at your front desk is critical to the first impression because they are the ones that have the first contact with the client.

The front desk staff needs to be friendly, look great, and, ideally, have outgoing personalities that will pamper, pamper and pamper your clients. They should offer to take the client' s coat and then offer the client coffee, tea, water, a magazine, or a snack. They should ensure your clients are comfortable while they wait for their appointment.

The staff must be warm, inviting, and friendly, making the client feel that she is important and you are more than glad she is there.

Hopefully a goal you have established for your salon is to become an on-time machine where your clients are not waiting for scheduled appointments. So, after your front staff has greeted your client well, your stylist will now be ready to enthusiastically greet the client. At this time, your stylist should always give each client a thorough consultation, even when that client is a regular customer.

During the consultation, the stylist should always bring the client up-to-date on new trends to try. So many times we miss the opportunity to keep our regular clients feeling special. We fall into a rut with them, asking them each time they come in, "same as last time?" Instead you should say, "When I was looking at the up-and-coming new trends, I saw a hairstyle that I was thinking would look fabulous on you." How much better can you make a client feel than to tell her you think about her even when she is not in the salon?

It is very important to keep your current clients happy and feeling just as special as your new clients. The number one reason why clients leave is that they begin to feel like second-class citizens. You need to make every client feel she is the most special person and the most appreciated person in the world at that moment. Take advantage of the consultation each and every time. It is one of the most missed opportunities by salon professionals today.

Last, it is in the element of surprise that you will get the attention of the customer. You must create an experience that is memorable and different from your competition. Remember now, your first step was to know your competition, and by visiting your competition you can find out the vital information you need to set yourself apart.

So create an experience that is different and above and beyond your clients' expectations. For example:

- You may want to try offering free haircuts on your client's birthday.

- Pamper them with complimentary neck and head massages or a luxurious hand massage.

- Offer a complimentary car service for your elderly client or other client in desperate need of transportation.

- Offer to order lunch in from a nearby restaurant. We would cater this option to the professional woman or man whose tight schedule would not permit them to get their hair done during their lunch hour.

- After a chemical service, offer a free mini makeup application to compliment a client's new hairstyle and allow her to continue with the rest of her day looking great.

- It only takes a few minutes to do quick makeup, your clients will love it, and you can even take the opportunity to promote your makeup line.

The ideas are endless; be creative, and have fun with it!

I used to remind my staff to treat their best customers better. While all guests deserve to receive the best possible customer service, your regular clients should consistently receive special offers, loyalty programs, and appreciation events. That something extra will encourage your clients to come back, and it is a way of saying "thank you."

"Thank you" is such an important phrase for customer loyalty. Essentially, every "thank you" says "I appreciate your business, and I will not take it for granted." It is just as powerful whether it's delivered in person or in an email. Always remember to let your clients know you are thankful to have them as a customer. Who wouldn't like this kind of gratitude?

Don't forget to keep in mind how your salon and staff are being seen from the client's perspective. Put yourself in their shoes at all times. Is there any inappropriate or unprofessional conversation occurring? Is your client being ignored while your stylists are chatting to each other? I have witnessed so many stylists yelling across the room for their client to go to the sink area and she will meet them there.

In the next section I go further into this subject and offer specific steps you should be taking to make all of your clients happy campers.

I will also guide you through the steps that will make your salon promotions fun and still keep them cost effective.

So remember, if you pamper your client, making her feel as special as you can, you are already ahead of the game. Your salon image and the professionalism of your staff are extremely important. Something Dale Carnegie once said has stuck with me for years: "The rare individual who unselfishly tries to serve others has an enormous advantage -- he has very little competition."

Individual Worksheet Exercise

Is your salon at the top of its game? Yes_____No_____

Are your current clients receiving a consultation before every service? Yes_____No_____

Are you successful in bringing new services to existing clients? Yes_____No_____

Is your front desk staff friendly, do they have outgoing personalities, and do they pamper, pamper, and pamper your clients? Yes_____No_____Somewhat_____

Are your clients offered coffee, tea, water, a snack, and/or a magazine? Yes_____No_____

Do your customers have to wait more than a few minutes for their appointments? Often_____Sometimes_____Rarely_____

From your clients' perspective while they are in your salon:

- Is there any inappropriate or unprofessional conversation occurring? Yes_____ No_____

- Are your stylists chatting to one another and ignoring their clients? Yes_____ No_____

- Do your stylists ever yell across the room for their clients to go to the sink area and they will meet them there? Yes_____No_____

- Do your stylists always keep a clean working environment and ready for their next client? Yes_____No_____

- Do your stylists leave their customer unattended while they are getting a chemical service? Yes_____No_____

It All Begins With the First Impression

Impressions are made in the first_____seconds of entering the salon.

When a new client comes into your salon, how do you think he/she would rate each of the following?

(Circle the number, on a scale of 1-10, with 1 being "poor" and 10 being "the absolute best"):

Front Desk	1	2	3	4	5	6	7	8	9	10
Receptionist	1	2	3	4	5	6	7	8	9	10
Waiting Area	1	2	3	4	5	6	7	8	9	10
Stylist Station	1	2	3	4	5	6	7	8	9	10
Stylist Image	1	2	3	4	5	6	7	8	9	10
Their Consultation	1	2	3	4	5	6	7	8	9	10
Shampoo Area	1	2	3	4	5	6	7	8	9	10
Retail Area	1	2	3	4	5	6	7	8	9	10
Salon Service received	1	2	3	4	5	6	7	8	9	10

HUSH! ROYALTY IS WALKING THROUGH THE DOOR!

SECTION TWO

CREATING LOYAL CLIENTS

In this chapter we will be covering promotions.

- You will learn several ways to create promotions that are fun for the client and also lucrative for your salon.

- You will learn how to separate your salon from the ho-hum-drum atmosphere that so many salons exude today.

- We will go over how to use your promotions to build loyal relationships with your clients that will keep them coming back.

- In my years of owning salons and training salon owners on how to be creative when developing promotions, I have seen salons be able to set up incentives for their staff, but I have seen very few that have successfully designed and offered programs for the client.

Having programs that are fun and save the customer money is a sure way to keep the client coming back.

And remember, remember, that excellent customer service will always set your business apart.

So let's take a look at some promotions that have proven to be highly successful.

Instead of cutting back in the slow economy, I used to offer complimentary services that my competition was not offering. Since clients were still spending their hard-earned money, I made sure every client got to experience luxury while they were in my salon.

For starters, I purchased a Keurig coffee machine with gourmet coffees, teas, and hot chocolate.

We also offered complimentary hand massages to clients who were waiting for a color to process or while they were getting a deep protein conditioner.

We offered complimentary bang trims for clients in between haircuts and complimentary detailing for men in between cuts.

We offered a complimentary color refresher service between color services to keep the color always looking great.

We used very little color and just did a little touch-up, but it made our clients very happy clients.

We offered complimentary lip gloss application and/or blush application after our cut and color services. Our clients loved leaving the salon with a little fresh makeup in addition to their new hairstyle.

We all know that the majority of salons charge extra for these services. So when you offer them as complimentary services, you will build client loyalty.

An added benefit is that other clients in the salon don't know some guests are there for a complimentary service; they only see a busy salon.

When I started implementing these promotions, I saw an increase in my client returns. And while they were there, some even purchased products or decided on another service.

It's a win-win situation for both the client and the salon.

Another win-win promotion is to offer incentives to get your client to buy professional products instead of drugstore hair care products.

I had the only salons in their areas that offered this incentive. My salons encouraged our clients to bring in any over-the-counter used or unused drugstore-brand hair care product from home and exchange it for 20% off any in-salon, retail purchase.

This ensured that our clients were using the best professional products possible. We then donated the unopened store products to our favorite charities, and yes, it is a nice tax write-off.

I am a firm believer in a 100% full credit back to clients if they don't like a product they've purchased. If a client ever returned a product, I allowed the client a store credit to use in any way she wanted in my salon. It makes a client so much more apt to buy retail knowing that there is a guarantee on all of the products.

Let's take a look at some other promotions.

The mystery envelope is a sure winner. In this promotion, the client receives an envelope with a certain percentage off the next visit. The client brings the unopened envelope to the appointment. After the service is completed, the envelope is opened and the percentage is taken off the total.

Have your clients save their receipts until they add up to a certain total (an amount preset by you) and then the client gets x amount off the next service.

Hold a makeover contest. Have clients and potential customers submit a photo with an explanation of what they would like changed and why. Then select several candidates to go through a complete makeover.

This is a great way to obtain e-mail addresses as well. You could also hold the makeover contest as a raffle.

Then during the makeover, have a photographer there to take before and after pictures. You can then use those photos in a portfolio showing off the work of your staff. Keep the portfolio in the reception area so that clients can easily browse through it.

Hook up with a local TV station and do makeovers on live TV.

Offer to do waitresses hair for free in your area to help advertise your salon services. They can wear a button with your salon's name on it.

To build your older clientele, go to a senior center where they offer all sorts of activities for the seniors. Arrange to go in and give a presentation on the services you offer. Bring gift certificates and hand them out to each senior.

Hold a seasonal hair/fashion show with a local boutique and promote each other's businesses.

Have a "Wacky Wednesday" offering a "Mommy and Me" special for a parent and child. With mom's haircut, the child's haircut is 50% off or free (it's whatever you choose).

Hold a "Be Treated Like a Queen Day." Offer a variety of package specials for your salon clientele and pamper them to death.

Start sending birthday cards to your clients.

Go through your lost client list and send them a "we miss you" card with a percentage off their next visit.

Hold 'tween' s birthday party bashes. Offer refreshments, manis and pedis, and get your hair done. This is very successful. It is lots of fun, and the kids will talk about it forever.

Have a different theme day where you all dress up for a certain theme. We dressed up for the Red Sox during the playoffs as a way of supporting many of the New England sports fans.

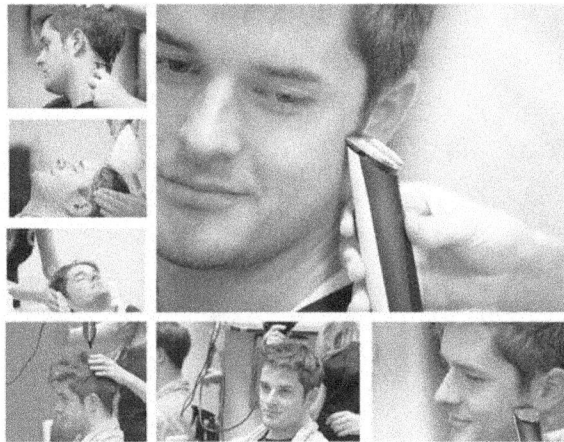

Host a "men' s night" and offer snacks and drinks. Put them through a wonderful tea tree experience where you heat up a towel (you can use hot water or a microwave if you don' t have a towel warmer) and either put the warm towel around the back of the neck or their facial area. Shampoo their hair after a soothing scalp massage with tea tree oil. Offer a shave as well, and this would be a great way to pamper your male clientele.

Give an on-time guarantee for professionals with tight schedules. Promise a big percentage off the total service bill if a client is waiting more than x number of minutes. This is a great gimmick, and it states the faith you have in running your salon in a smooth, on-time fashion.

Father-and-son days are always a blast. Offer something special with both their haircuts, such as a toy for the boy and a product for the father. This also opens a way for you to introduce products to your male clientele.

Offering a babysitting service is also a great way to differentiate yourself from your competition. How many times have we, as hairstylists, gritted our teeth while doing the parents hair and the parent is allowing the child to run wild. Then there are those parents that put off coming in because they don' t have babysitting available.

You can offer a "wish list" questionnaire. When a client first comes in, the receptionist could give a questionnaire to the client to fill out. The questionnaire should ask the client what would make the experience in your salon unforgettable. Give examples for her to circle or to write in. Then take this information and fulfill it.

Make sure your salon always has magazines geared for all your clientele: men, women, and children.

The following is a list of "Business Builder" promotions I utilize in some of my classes. A number of these suggestions we just went over, but there are additional ideas as well. There are so many promotions you can create to increase your business!

BUSINESS BUILDERS

1. **Makeover Contest:** Have clients and potential customers submit a photo and a sheet explaining what they would like to change and why. Select several candidates to go through a complete makeover. Have a photographer on hand to capture the moment.

2. **Gift with Purchase:** This is where a client receives a free gift with a minimum investment.

3. **Purchase with Purchase:** This idea has been successfully used by most major cosmetic companies. A product travel kit or tote bag with your logo could be purchased by your client at a savings.

4. **Yearly Coupon Cards:** Select twelve items you would like to give away for a year. One card is printed with small boxes, one for each month, stating the free

gift and the value. "With any $27.00 service, you may redeem the coupon for your free gift from our company."

5. **Free Service with a Service:** Cross merchandising services to your clients is crucial. Try offering a complimentary manicure with each perm or a facial for each new color client. Use your imagination to create other combinations.

6. **Product of the Month:** Select one product to be featured each month. Allow for extra display space and have fact sheets available for clients to read, along with proper signage.

7. **Spoil Yourself Rotten:** Try a campaign for those clients who need to get away from it! A half-day package works best: facial, manicure, body massage and make-up – and remember the cappuccino.

8. **Save Your Receipts:** One salon owner in Virginia has all of her clients save their receipts and when they total $200, the client receives $25 in free service.

9. **Bridal Package:** Put together a complete beauty program for the bride. Facials, hair, make-up, manicure, pedicure and waxing – make-up on the day of the wedding for the bride and maid of honor, all for one set price.

10. **Buy One Get One Free:** Service or product.

11. **Buy One Get One for a Penny:** Service or product.

12. **Mystery Envelopes:** One of our local department stores sponsors a mystery envelope promotion every year. The store's customer is mailed a sealed envelope with a card enclosed for 10-90% off. The envelope is presented unopened to the clerk when you check out. You receive the percentage discount on your purchase.

13. **Gift Certificates:** These should be displayed year-round. Frame one and display it in each of your treatment rooms.

14. **Giveaways:** Many radio stations are looking for gifts that can be given to listeners in exchange for on-air promotions. You can get your salon's name out over the airwaves without buying ad time.

15. **Career Looks:** Circulate flyers among graduating high school and college students. Start your promotion in March. Many graduates will then request a gift certificate as a graduation present.

16. **Fund Raisers:** The types of service you offer make enticing gifts as door prizes at auctions and school raffles. Make a list of the organizations that you would like to support for the year and the total amount budgeted to fund raisers.

17. **Hook up with a Local TV Station:** Do makeovers on live TV.

18. **Build Your Older Clientele:** Arrange to go to a senior center, where they offer activities for seniors, and give a presentation on the services you offer. Bring gift certificates and hand them out to each senior.

19. **Offer to do Waitresses Hair for Free in Your Area:** In return, have them wear a button with your salon's name on it to advertise your salon services.

20. **Hold 'Tweens Birthday Party Bashes:** Offer refreshments, manis, pedis, and get your hair done. It is lots of fun, and the kids will talk about it forever.

21. **Offer VIP Cards to Military Personnel:** They can keep the card in their wallet to use when they come to your salon, offering them a discount, such as 15% off their haircuts.

22. **Attract Your Local Medical Personnel:** Put together special packages for nurses and medical staff at the hospitals and clinics near you.

23. **Make up VIP Cards for Students:** Hand them out to all your teenage clients to give to their friends.

Even with your fabulous promotions and outstanding customer service, you will occasionally have a client with a complaint. Always take any complaints from you clientele seriously. You can turn these complaints around to be a positive learning experience. Share the information with the staff and together you can change the negative into something positive. An apology letter to the disgruntled client could go a long way to soothe the savage beast.

Years ago I remember, after having a visit with a dentist, that he called me the next day to see how I was doing. I was very impressed and felt so special. Use this method after a client comes in for the first time, or you can also use it with your regular clients. Call them up after their color or chemical service to see if they were pleased.

This could give you an opportunity to be able to correct an issue when the client is unhappy.

Some clients won' t ever complain; they just won' t come back. However, if they are asked directly, once they are away from the salon, they might be willing to tell you that they were displeased. By acting preemptively, you can apologize and invite them back for a free service or to redo their hair to their satisfaction. In this way, you can avoid a lost client.

The key information to take from here today is that it is an ongoing process whereby you need to continuously try to define why a client should come to your salon and not your competition. And you need to keep on asking and answering that question again and again and again.

Throughout my travels, I have picked up many little sayings, and I thought I would sum up this chapter by sharing a few of my favorites with you.

⭐⭐⭐ *Little Sayings* ⭐⭐⭐

There is only one boss: the customer.

Your most unhappy customer is your best tool to learn from.

If we don' t take care of our customer, someone else will.

You never get a second chance to make a first impression.

Are you treating your client the way you would want to be treated?

Customer service is an attitude not a department.

What you talk about is what you will bring about.

The outcome of your life depends on what your thoughts consist of.

Your mind attracts what you think.

You can believe in God and know he can or you can KNOW God and believe He will.

The law of nature is the same for all of us. Please remember what you give out, you get back. No one has ever planted corn and gotten tomatoes. When we sow positive we reap positive.

We are fortunate to be in such a great industry where the sky is the limit for you to be able to differentiate yourself from all of your competition and bring success into your salon!

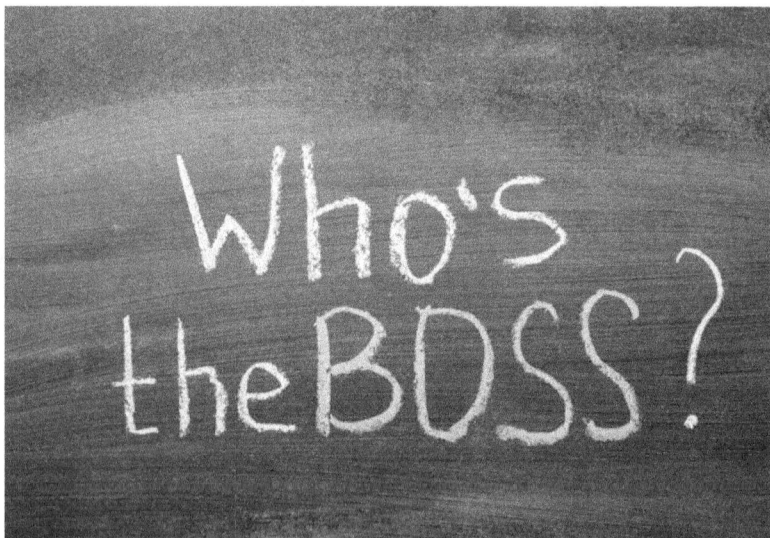

HUSH! ROYALTY IS WALKING
THROUGH THE DOOR!

SECTION THREE

RETAINING YOUR CLIENTS

Earlier in this chapter I quoted one of my favorite sayings by Dale Carnegie, which I feel merits mentioning again. He said, "The rare individual who unselfishly tries to serve others has an enormous advantage - he has very little competition."

How sad is this statement, especially for salon professionals who are in the business of serving others and making people feel better about themselves.

In this section, we will talk about how to give the most excellent customer service that will keep your clients coming back over and over again. So let's get started!

In my years of training salon owners, I have tried to impress upon them that if they take the time to figure out what it costs on average to get a new customer into the salon, it can help to put things into perspective. You may find that you spend quite a bit of money, and time, to obtain every new customer, and recognizing this fact makes it even more worth your effort to retain them. So what is the secret? Outrageous customer service.

Is your salon at the top of its game? Here are some strategies to help ensure that the clients you have now will be with you for the long haul.

The greeting of your client is so much more important than you think. Always greet your client with a big hello and a handshake or hug if it is in your comfort level. Guide her back to your station and hold the chair for her while she sits down. The consultation should begin. You want to listen intently while she talks about her hair. Do not speak to her through the mirror; it is much more personal to talk face-to-face with her during the consultation.

Although it is a stylist's goal to be booked at all times, I have seen many stylists fall into the same rut of becoming complacent, especially with regular clients. So if a regular client comes in and suggests she is ready to try something different, never, ever, regardless of how busy you are, say, "No." Take time with her and go over all the details of what she is looking for.

Many of us feel that we know exactly what to do with a frequent client without even asking. We believe we know best what the client really wants, and that she doesn't really want a change. THIS IS A BIG MISTAKE!!!!! It's important that you know what's going on with your regular clients, each and every visit. We need to be open to anything our client is telling us and find ways to keep her looking and feeling great and never taken for granted!

One of the keys to maintaining a loyal clientele is to look for ways to bring new services to existing clients. The stylist should always start each consultation by listening to the wants and needs of the client. Next, the stylist should repeat back to the client what was just said to make sure the stylist fully understands what she has heard.

This is your chance now to make suggestions based on your expertise, and here lies the opportunity to suggest a few exciting ideas. Normally, these suggestions should be linked to the latest styling trends in cut and color that can be added to the service your client wants. If you have a client who gets regular cuts but currently isn't receiving color services, make use of your consultation time to talk about what she does and does not like about her hair and her hair color. If she expresses concern about going grey or hints that her hair is looking a little lifeless, take it as an opportunity to suggest different options she could do to remedy the situation. If she is unsure or hesitant, you can suggest she think about it.

Your suggestions will have planted a seed in her mind that then allows you to take it a step further the next time she comes in. You can suggest a color change that is still close to her original color, but with just enough difference to boost shine and dimension. You will most likely end up with a dedicated cut and color client, one who changes her look regularly based on your expert advice. Your client won't get bored and will find she is looking at her friend and saying, "I love your hair, where do you get it done?"

If <u>you</u> are not updating your client and making new suggestions, she will try another salon looking for the change that you have not been telling her about.

Personally, I learned this lesson when I was a young stylist working in Florida where the snow birds would leave for the summer and come back for the winter. A couple of my clients came back one winter with totally different hairstyles and color. They raved about their summer stylist and how she had shown them some great new styles; styles that were the newest trend and that she thought would look great on them. I remember being very impressed, and I saw first-hand the importance of always treating your existing clients with the same excitement and respect that you would your new clients.

So, you need to get with the times, and get your staff into this century. Utilize the internet. It is a great tool for viewing pictures of your client's favorite celebrity's hairstyle and color.

You can upload a portfolio of the newest trends, cuts, color, and makeover images on your laptop or tablet and browse through the pictures in your consultation with your client. Imagine how special your client will feel when you're prepared to show her several styles that you think she would look great in. She'll know you were thinking about her, and that you value the importance of giving her a style she'll love.

Throughout my years of extensive traveling in this business, I have seen very few instances where the customer service was so special that the client was willing to wait a period of time for a certain stylist. The very few times I have seen this, I asked the client what it was that enabled her to not mind a long wait for a particular stylist. The response always revolved around the fact that the stylist made her feel special, that when she got into the stylist's chair, she felt like the most valued person alive, and she knew she would have the stylist's undivided attention.

In my observations, the most successful salons are the ones that have a talented and dedicated group of staff who work together, in sync, as a team. Teach your stylists that they should always take the opportunity to be kind to everyone else's clients, and that they are responsible for ensuring that all the other clients who come to the salon feel just as special as their own.

Unfortunately, though, no matter how talented your staff is, there will always be the occasional unhappy client. Remember that most clients don't complain. Instead, they just don't come back.

Make sure your guest feels comfortable communicating with you and expressing exactly how he or she feels about your services. I have seen all too often the situation where a client is lost because the stylist made her feel afraid to express her true feelings about her hair.

I highly suggest a phone call to all clients that have received a new service or style. This will let them know that you do care about keeping them happy. It can also give you an opportunity to head off any potential problems. If for any reason they did not like their hair, you can invite them back in to fix it. There is great power in making a client feel special, and creating that special feeling is our mission.

When you have an unhappy client, you still need to treat that client like royalty, regardless of whether she lets you know she is unhappy at the time of the service or whether she comes back later to tell you. I have seen many instances where a client is displeased with her hair for whatever reason, and the stylist has gotten defensive, arguing with the client that she did exactly what she asked her to do.

This attitude is so dangerous.

For starters, it puts the client into a fight-back mode, whether she actually gets into a disagreement with the stylist or she simply leaves and never comes back. You must remember that the client is always right.

If she isn' t happy, you need to fix whatever it is that will make her happy. Remember, you have one boss: the client. She has the ability to fire you at any time by spending her money at your competition. So stylists, swallow your pride and with great empathy, converse with your client to determine what she really wants.

If a client comes back to the salon, after-the-fact, to complain about her hair, the manager or owner needs to step in. Again, it horrifies me how many times I have witnessed stylists responding to a client with such phrases as, "I don' t know who handles this," "I can' t help you because I am busy," "come back later," or "your hair looks fine to me;" the list of inappropriate things that have been said is endless. You can imagine how irate this makes the client. Instead, always diffuse her anger with statements such as "I am so sorry you had to come all the way back," or "I certainly can understand your frustration, and we will take care of the situation." Such statements will not only validate her anger but will also allow her to communicate with you in a more normal tone now. Then you can say things like, "I would be happy to help you with this," or "let' s take a look at some options that would make you happier with your hair."

So, remember that the opinions of your clients should always be taken seriously. I am a firm believer that, if you are willing to listen, your customers can give you the best advice for your business. They can be your biggest fans or your harshest critics.

I suggest that even when they are not volunteering feedback to you, ask them how you are doing and what they like about your salon and what they don't like. Feel free to send them a gift certificate to use in your salon as a thank you for their input.

Work together with your staff, as a team, to improve any areas that need improvement because good customer service is a team sport. It was a priority in my salons that my stylists were all educated in the importance of outrageous customer service. You must create an experience that is different and beyond your clients' expectations. For example:

- Offer umbrellas for your clients to use when it is raining then walk them to their car.

- Offer free snacks and drinks. You can put a small refrigerator with a glass door in your salon and fill it with miniature-sized water bottles and juice bottles for clients to help themselves.

- Each of my clients always received a birthday card and a Christmas card.

- For my female professional women, I had a chilled glass of wine waiting for them after work and pampered them with a neck and scalp massage before their service.

Lots of salons offer this value-added massage service, so what makes it so special? It is the stylist. A massage is meant to relax and calm your client, not make her feel uncomfortable.

Instead of performing the massage like a robot, put some thought into what you're doing and really work to make it a special experience for your client. What a wonderful way to end the day.

The ideas are limitless; just think of what you would like if you were the client and have fun with it! Remember, your client is royalty. Treat them as such, and you will have a dedicated following.

Dealing with Unhappy Customers

What can get a customer upset enough not to return to your salon?

1.

2.

3.

4.

5.

List positive ways to deal with a disgruntled client:

1.

2.

3.

4.

5.

Make a list of phrases that you WOULD and WOULD NOT say when dealing with an upset client.

DO Say

1.

2.

3.

4.

5.

6.

DON'T Say

1.

2.

3.

4.

5.

The Unexpected Customer Service

What do clients **EXPECT** for customer service in your salon?

1.

2.

3.

4.

5.

What do you think your clients' **UNEXPECTED** expectations might be?

1.

2.

3.

4.

5.

Let's say there are 10 salons in a three mile radius of your salon, and the average number of stylists in each of these salons are 10. Therefore, there are 100 reasons clients don't need to come to your salon. This verifies the importance of outshining your competition.

Action Plan

My **goals** for creating experiences that are memorable for my clients are:

1.

2.

3.

4.

5.

6.

The **steps (action plan) I can implement** in my salon in order to reach my goals of going above and beyond my customers' expectations are:

1.

2.

3.

4.

5.

6.

CHAPTER THREE

RETAILING IN ACTION

RETAILING IN ACTION

SECTION ONE

COMPASSIONATE RETAILING

What thoughts come to your mind when you hear the word retailing? Jot them down before going forward.

Are your thoughts about retailing positive or negative? Why?

Many stylists reject retailing because they see it as "selling" instead of another means of helping their client.

These salon professionals don't realize that selling retail products should come as naturally to them as selling clients a style, color, or cut which they do every day!

In this section:

- I will go over the importance of re- tailing for salon professionals and explain why it is such a crucial component of building a strong client base.

- I will give step-by-step instructions outlining how to conduct a successful consultation in order to get clients to talk about issues they are having with their hair. I will then show you how to give your clients solutions to all of their hair concerns.

- I will also explain the importance of up-selling services to your clients, making them aware of all the options they have to change their hair if they desire.

So let's get started!

Professionals who think that they are not sales people are mistaken. They sell their skills, their talents, and their knowledge every day, in every way.

Keep in mind that we stylists must give our clients reasons why they NEED certain products. Therefore, you have to know what you are selling. You must be educated on the product. You should use it your-

self. It is important to have first- hand knowledge of how the product works so that you know its benefits. It's hard to sell something you don't understand. Here are 10 step-by-step points to help you conquer the difficulties with retailing that so many salons experience.

1. After a client has been greeted and is seated in your chair, the consultation should begin.

2. You should request the client's per- mission to ask a few questions about her hair before you get started.

3. At this point, you can begin to ask probing questions that would make it easy for the client to tell the history of her hair. Ask the client what she has done in the past that she liked and what she did not like. Ask the client what she likes about her current hair- style and what she is happy with and does not want changed.

It is extremely important to allow the client to tell you what issues and problems she is having with her hair. What you are doing is getting the CLIENT to tell you what is wrong with her hair

instead of insulting her by YOU telling her what is wrong with her hair. This tactic is much more diplomatic, and she will respect you much more with this approach. Essentially, you are asking permission from the client for you to discover information about her hair from her, so she, in turn, will be more apt to listen to your response, expertise and knowledge.

What questions will you ask to help your client feel comfortable sharing with you? How will you help your client open up?

4. At this point, you will want to ask the client, "If there was anything you could change about your hair what would it be?

Often times, clients don't realize all the options that we, as hairstylists, have to offer. I make this part of the question- ing a fun game, and I may pretend to be a genie, who can grant the client 5 wishes, without limitations, to change her hair.

"More volume," "shinier hair," "straight and less frizzy," "healthy looking hair," "more texture in my hair," are just a few of the many things a client might suggest about her hair to you.

What other ways could you help your client think of changes?

Now you should repeat back what the client has told you to verify you heard everything correctly.

5. After the client agrees that you heard correctly, here is your chance to offer options that will help fix the problems the client has just listed.

This is an opportunity for you to explain the different services offered at the salon and all the different options available to the client to help her with her hair concerns.

For example, I had a variety of menus in my salon reception area that explained the different services we offered. Many times clients were not even aware of these services. If the client mentioned to me that she was having hair volume issues, I would bring her our texture menu to show and explain all the different options we offered for volumizing and style support without having to go curly.

If the client complained about dull, frizzy hair, I would go over our menu choices for re- texturizing hair and explain all the options and services we offered to take care of the problem. At the end of this workbook, I have included examples of the texture menus I offered in my salons, so feel free to look them over for ideas.

Be sure not to overwhelm the client with too many things at once. The idea is to educate her about the different solutions you can offer her and plant a seed for her next visit.

6. Once you have finished with this portion of the consultation, you then want to ask the client what products she is currently using. If the client answers with a drug store brand, don't gasp, just gently tell the client that you will be using "such-and-such" products today, and that they will help with the hair concerns the client has explained. Remember stylists: you are not selling a product, you are selling a solution!

How is selling a solution better than selling a product?

7. Next, when the client moves to the shampoo bowl, you should remind her of the issue with her hair that was dis cussed during the consultation. For example, let's say the client mentioned that her hair lacked volume, then you would want to briefly say, "I 11 using our volumizing shampoo and conditioner." Then give her the best scalp massage ever. She will be greatly appreciative

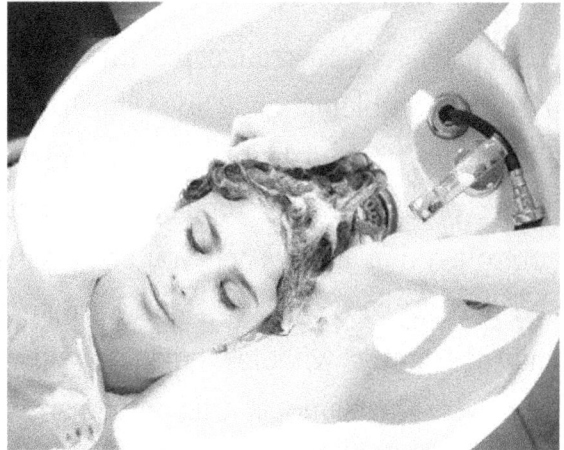

8. When the client gets back to the chair, you will then begin the service. When you are applying product, you should be sure that it coincides with the issue the client shared about her hair. For example you should say, "I will be using this shine product that will help to de-frizz your hair and give you great shine."

During the service, you should take the time to educate your client on how to use each product and let her hold the products as you are using them. This enables the client to feel ownership of the products she is holding.

9. And finally, after the service is complete, you should go to the shelves and pick out the products you used on your client and set them up in front of the client. This is the time to review the products with the client. If the client suggests she cannot purchase them all, for whatever reason, you should recommend the most important ones to get her started.

Remember stylists, your client is a walking billboard for you. You want to make sure she knows how to obtain the style as well as you do. This is especially true if the style is new to her.

You need to keep in mind, if you, the stylist, don't know the problem, how can you give a solution? All this points to the importance of stylists knowing the science of hair and knowing products and their ingredients so they can prescribe the right antidote.

A stylist needs to realize the important role that professional products play in addressing hair problems and how much more effective they are than drug store brands. Chemically treated hair can often times be dry and fragile, especially if the client isn't taking precautions by replacing the nutrients that the chemicals remove. This is called controlled damage. When you chemically treat hair, its natural proteins are depleted and need to be replaced by the right product. For example, if you go to the bank and constantly withdraw money without making any deposits, you will be in the negative. The same is true with hair. If you are depleting without replacing, the hair will eventually not be able to tolerate any chemical services until the hair is repaired. Most clients automatically believe that when their hair feels dry and brittle, they need moisture. Most often that is exactly what they don't need. Adding moisture may only add to the problem.

Protein is what will help to rebuild the hair back into a healthy state. I can't tell you how many salon professionals do not know this.

I studied Trico analysis (the study of hair) for years and be- came very knowledge-able about what hair needs and what to look for when determining the right product for people to use. Porosity and elasticity of the hair are two crucial parts to take into consideration when determining the damage of the hair and what can be done to restore it to health.

Scenario 1: Ellen's hair is breaking and feels like a scouring pad. Every time she combs or brushes her hair, pieces of hair snap and break off. Her hair feels hard and rough even when it is wet. She has been getting protein treatments because her stylist told her the protein is sup- posed to stop breakage and will help to rebuild the hair. She is using a professional fortifying protein shampoo and conditioner at home. But so far, nothing is working and her problem is getting worse.

Scenario 2: Nancy's hair also has a lot of breakage. Her hair feels dry, brittle, looks dull, and is very weak. When her hair is combed when it is wet, it stretches like a rubber band and then breaks. Her hair lacks shine and body and appears limp with no life at all. She is getting moisturizing treatments from her stylist. Since her breakage began, she has started getting these treatments weekly and follows it up with a professional hydrating shampoo and conditioner, but her problem has gotten worse.

I can't tell you how many times over the years I have seen stylists recommending the wrong products, a.k.a. the wrong solution, resulting in a client's hair not being treated properly. Most of the time, the client will blame the product. This is why it is so important the stylist knows what to prescribe.

In scenario 1, the problem is that Ellen's hair needs a higher concentrate of hydrating treatments and products. Ellen should be using a professional hydrating shampoo and conditioner to help solve her problem.

In scenario 2, Nancy's hair needs a higher concentration of protein in her home maintenance products. In addition, she would benefit from in-salon deep protein treatments.

So how does the stylist manually tell the difference? Wet the hair, take a strand of hair between your two fore fingers and wrap the hair around each finger. Now pull. If the hair stretches like a rubber band and then breaks, this is a good indicator that the hair needs protein. If the hair does not have any pull and return or flexibility and feels hard and rough when it is wet, this is a good indicator that the hair needs moisturizing treatments.

To test for porosity of the hair, take a wet strand of hair between your thumb and fore finger and slide up the hair shaft towards the root of the hair. If the hair has a rough feel to it, this means the cuticle is open and the hair is very porous. If your fingers glide more smoothly along the hair shaft, this means the cuticle is more intact. If the hair is more porous, it is a good indicator that the hair most likely may need protein.

If the hair is very elastic and is mushy when wet this is a good indicator that the hair will need more protein. If the hair is dry and feels hard and rough when wet this is a good indicator that the hair needs more moisture.

What I have been describing here are just a few additional tests you can use when you are trying to determine the overall condition of your client's hair.

Protein and moisture work together synergistically to produce a healthy head of hair, and neither can work well without the other. Keeping the hair balanced between these two entities is very important. Achieving the proper balance involves using the right combinations of protein and moisture based on what the hair needs.

When clients shop in a drugstore, they will not have the professional opinion that a hairstylist can provide about what their hair is lacking and what it needs. They often just grab a product advertising what they THINK their hair needs without actually KNOWING what their hair needs. This information can only come from a salon professional.

Professional products contain different forms of protein that are broken down and absorbed by the hair. Drug store brands don't always contain the same types of protein as professional products. Professional products also contain the right balance of vitamins and moisturizing elements which are important for healthy hair. Drug store brands may not always contain the same ingredients in the same composition; therefore, they may be cheaper but are not always beneficial to the hair.

You can use your expertise to educate your clients about the superior ingredients in your products over those found in drug stores. Then they will understand why your products are a little more expensive. They may cost more to buy, but they produce the desired results. Your clients can stop searching for a bar- gain priced solution that doesn' t exist.

Choosing products to use and sell in your salon is very important and needs to be supported by your salon team. You must choose products and companies in which you believe. So ask yourselves, "Do we believe in these products and love the results they produce?"

"Do we love the look, feel and smell of the products?" Remember clients of- ten buy on scent alone. You also need to ask yourselves, "Do the products we sell give fabulous results the very first time we use them on clients?" It is important that you choose products that you truly believe are the best for your clients be- cause they should also be the products you use yourself.

What products can you confidently recommend to your clients right now?

_____

_____

_____

_____

What products should you consider adding to those in your salon?

_____

_____

_____

_____

Successful retailing in the salon will elevate you from an average stylist to a dynamic one. Your customers will appreciate your knowledge. They will appreciate you for taking the time to show them how to duplicate their styles at home with the right professional products.

As a stylist, imagine how difficult it would be for you to not use any styling products; imagine just using water to try to create a perfect style in your hair.

Remember···········.

Know all you can about the products you are prescribing.

Use the products yourself and familiarize yourself with all their benefits and how they work for you.

Always establish a need by listening and asking questions throughout your client's service.

Describe to your clients the products' features and how they will benefit their hair. Be sure you address any hair issues your client has told you about.

Demonstrate the use of the product on your clients. Educate them on how to do it at home.

Involve your customers with the product. Let them hold it, smell it, and feel its consistency. Show them the amount of the product they will be using. Over doing will end up with bad results, and clients will blame the product saying it makes their hair greasy, flat, etc.

Make the decision that you will suggest and recommend product to each and every one of your clients, old and new.

Keep this in mind: **If you don't ask your clients to purchase products, someone else will.**

Remember, talking to clients about their hair is a priority. Do not start off their visits by asking them about their love life or their social status. Talk about hair.

If you talk about, demonstrate, and educate your clients on their hair and the different products that will benefit them, they will love it. There will be plenty of time to chat about the other things later when they come back again and again.

Retailing is all about helping clients. It can make them feel better about the look they created. It will make them feel more confident. It will fix their hair dilemma, and they will think you are a genius.

When you look at retailing as helping someone find a solution, do you still feel like a salesperson? You are selling them product, yes, but only because it solves their problem. You only have the very best intentions.

Now we need to talk about retail goal set- ting. One way to start selling retail, would be by setting achievable goals that you can easily reach.

For example, one or two products per day would be attainable. You can gradually increase that number. It is amazing how quickly you can reach a goal of selling just one or two products to 50% of your clients daily.

What retailing goals will you set?

_____

_____

_____

_____

_____

When your retail sales are down, analyze what you are talking about with your clients. Change your approach a bit and stay focused on hair. It is amazing how easily this works. It is truly effortless when you actually care about your clients.

Selling retail in the hair industry is not "selling" if you are "helping." It is up to you to choose how helpful and considerate you want to be. In a world where so many people feel desperate to be heard and cared for, this compassionate retailing is a sure way to experience success.

RETAILING IN ACTION

SECTION TWO

OVERCOMING RETAILING AND
UP-SELL**ING** OBSTACLES

Would you like to know how to involve your stylists in retailing? Would you like to discover how elite resources in the industry overcome up-selling obstacles? Would you like to learn productive ways to assist your staff in retailing successfully?

In this chapter, I will include the tips and strategies that I have taught in my classes, and used in my own salons, that have proven to be the most successful. In addition,

I will cover promotions and incentive programs for successful retailing. So let's get started!

Here are some of the excuses I have heard from stylists about why they do not sell products, along with my responses to them.

1. **I am not a sales person.**

However, every time you, the stylist, suggest a style change or recommend a color service, you are selling your own taste, skills, and knowledge.

2. **I don't want to sound pushy.**

So don't push! Your clients come to you specifically for your advice and expertise. When they leave your chair they are looking their very best. It is important that you educate your clients on how to style their own hair and that you prescribe the right tools and products for clients to use at home; products that you have chosen specifically for their hair.

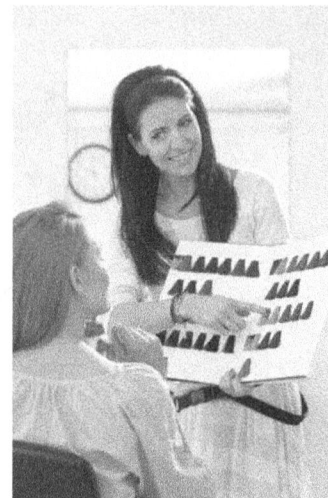

3. **The products are on display; if clients want something, they will buy it.**

As much as our staff would like to believe this statement, clients need a stylist's professional advice and guidance. An attractive display is important. It grabs a client's attention, but it doesn't provide clients with the knowledge of which products are best suited for their hair. Products do not sell themselves.

I'm afraid of selling.

I have always been a firm believer that the antidote to fear is knowledge. The more comfortable and knowledgeable you are, the more confident you will be in selling.

4. **They won't buy no matter what I do.**

I can't tell you how many times I have heard stylists say this. Then when I watch them with a client they talk about everything other than product. Then at the end of the service, the stylist will say, "Are you all set with products?" If stylists are not explaining the products that they are using, and they don't establish a need with a client for the client to be using particular products, then they will NOT get the client to buy. I always told my staff, "You are selling a solution, not a product."

Successful retailing doesn't just happen. It is important for salon owners to learn how to prepare their stylists to sell.

What excuses have you heard? How have you responded to them?

_____

_____

_____

_____

When owners set out to discuss retail with their stylists, they need to be aware that it is much more involved than just having a stylist sell product. There are many things an owner can do to help a stylist feel more excited and secure when selling a product.

First and foremost, a salon must carry products that will motivate and excite both staff and clients.

Once you have chosen products, be sure you provide adequate training for your staff. I cannot emphasize this strongly enough. Knowledge of a product brings confidence and is crucial in order for a stylist to feel comfortable selling. Many manufacturers offer product knowledge education classes as a complimentary service.

If the stylist is aware of all the benefits and features of a product, she will be more apt to sell.

It is also important that the stylist uses the products in her own hair. I used to send my stylists home with different products to use themselves each week so they could become acquainted with all the products we stocked.

To be successful with retailing, it is essential to invite everyone on your team to be part of the process. As always, it starts with education. Remember, you should work with a company that will provide staff members with the training they need to understand their products inside and out. Talk with your staff about what products they like and what products they don' t like. It' s a team effort.

One incentive for selling that I used, in conjunction with my product companies, was to hold stylist sales competitions.

These always bring out the competitive spirit in everyone; so create weekly and monthly sales contests to motivate your stylists to sell. I would ask my sales consultant, from each distributorship I used, to provide some fabulous prizes for the contest winners; prizes that would bring excitement to the staff such as blow dryers or thermal irons. Other examples of prizes I would offer were a "Night on the Town" or gift certificates to a particular store or restaurant.

Another retail incentive program that was extremely popular with my staff was one I called "Celebrate the Small Stuff."

This program actually tripled my retail sales in less than three months. I am a strong believer in using positive reinforcements to motivate my staff, rather than negative consequences. So let me share with you my "secret formula."

1. Provide Constant and Consistent Focus.

- I would have my entire staff meet once a month to re- view their goals and to celebrate all the successes of my staff.

- I would meet with, or call, the salon manager three times a week to discuss goals and to review which staff members were achieving them and which of the staff needed more coaching.

- I would meet with, or make weekly phone calls to, each staff member, either coaching them on, or praising them for, what they had achieved. I made sure to be only encouraging, avoiding any negativity.

2. Have Robust Stylist Incentive Plans.

I put together stylist incentive plans that provided stylists with the opportunity to make bonuses of up to 25% of their monthly retail sales. For example:

- When any of my stylists sold up to $100 of product in a month, they received a 10% com- mission check.

- When stylists sold between $100-$200 of product in a month, they received a 15% commission check.

- When stylists sold over $200 and up to $1,200 of product in a month, they would receive a 20% commission check.

- When stylists sold over $1,200 of product in a month, they would receive a 25% commission check.

3. Have a Manager's Incentive Plan (based on monthly goals).

- The manager would receive $200 if 50% of the stylists met their retail goals.

- The manager would receive $300 if 100% of the stylists met their retail sales goals.

- The manager would receive an additional $200 if the salon had a 20% increase for the same month from the prior year in chemical sales.

I always made a very big deal of handing out incentive checks to my staff!

4. Set up Special Incentive Plans.

- I often took advantage of the holiday season to help my staff with their holiday shopping. I would put together fun games, such as giving stylists play money if they surpassed their specific goal. This play money was banked away for that stylist to "spend" on education, hair shows, or tools. It was a great way to encourage stylists to build a nest egg for special events. It taught them how to budget their money as well, which is something I found to be necessary in this profession.

- Any time stylists doubled their sales over the prior week, they received a $10 gift card to a local coffee shop. Even a little praise can go a long way.

- This next program was very successful at fostering healthy competition between my stylists:

- Three times a year, I would split my staff into teams. The team that sold the most products in a specified month would get a steak dinner. The team that lost got pizza. I always wanted to promote the feeling of winning for everyone.

5. Track Sales.

Tracking sales is very important and should be set up in a highly visible area in the back room for all your staff to view. Use any kind of chart such as a thermometer, map, dartboard, race (such as a steeple chase, see **Figure 1** be- low), or any other visual aid that has start and end points and moveable pieces so that the chart can be used to follow each stylist's success.

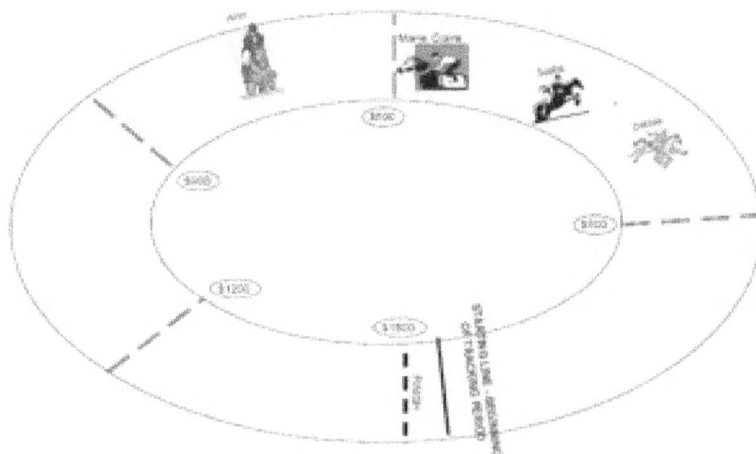

Figure 1. Example of a steeple chase chart.

Track your staff's sales by the week or month and celebrate each success!

Remember, the keys to keeping your staff focused on r e t a i l ing in your salon are:

1. Constant and continued focus.

2. Fair and equitable base incentive plans for stylists and managers.

3. Special incentive plans for stretch goals.

4. Setting and measuring weekly and monthly targets.

5. Celebrate each and every success, no matter how big or small.

6. Praise goes a long, long way.

I also used vacation vouchers as retailing incentives as I went over earlier in this book.

I had terrific success utilizing these vacation vouchers as stylist incentives. For example, I would give a certificate to stylists who sold over $x amount of retail during a month or special promotion. You can also give them to your stylists as a holiday gift.

I saw a significant increase in sales because my team was motivated to out-perform. I also found the certificates were a perk that enabled me to more easily retain my

top performers. Because I believe so strongly in these certificates, I offer them directly on my website. For more information and to learn how to purchase these incentive certificates, go to www.PositiveSalonStrategies.com and click on "Vacation Certificates."

Which of the retailing incentive programs you have just read would you like to try first?

_____

_____

_____

_____

What other retailing incentive programs will you create?

_____

_____

_____

Although products don't sell themselves, as I mentioned earlier, an attractive display of your products is important. Salon owners should step back and look at their retail shelves with the eyes of a client.

Don't hesitate to move things around the salon to create an ideal setup in all the areas of your salon. Your retail shelves should be very inviting so that the client will want to look through the products.

Many stores often change their displays on a regular basis. I used this method in my salons. If you don't change things up, the client will soon become oblivious to her surroundings when entering your salon.

Let your windows also do advertising for your salon.

Dress up the window with product sales, product of the month, and displays to go with the season or the holiday. Hanukkah, Christmas, Valentine's Day, Easter, Thanksgiving are among the many opportunities you have to dress up your windows. Let the window tell a story.

A customer will immediately know that you are also a retail salon.

Support your staffs' retailing efforts by getting the word out to your customers, too.

Many companies can assist with tools such as posters, shelf talkers, and displays of the products you have purchased from them. Make sure you utilize these materials. Usually they are complimentary! Place new products on styling stations to kick-start conversations between your stylist and customer. Use the stylists' stations for product specials and any other ideas that will help the stylist to remember to talk product.

Don' t forget the 100% satisfaction guarantee. Satisfied customers are the foundation of any business. This policy really helped my staff to feel more comfortable about selling new product to clients because they knew the client could always bring it back for an in-store credit or an exchange for another product. All products should be guaranteed, and you only want the very best products for your business. My salon guaranteed everything we sold because we firmly believed in the products that we carried.

Look around your salon. What are the best locations for pro- motional materials, displays and products to be placed?

So let's look at some other ways to have fun and help your stylists to stay focused on selling retail. The added bonus is that these tips are designed to be financially rewarding as well.

- Try to create promotional packages for various products each month. I used to create a theme for each promotion, usually centering the theme around the season, holidays and special occasions.

JANUARY is a great month to START THE NEW YEAR WITH A NEW YOU.

This advertises to clients that change is always available for their hair, skin, and nails. This month can be a slow-down month for retail since it comes right after the holidays. There- fore, it is an especially good time to create incentive retail programs for your stylists and incentive purchasing programs for your clients. For example, you could offer a facial and total makeup

make-over and offer $25.00 worth of product free. If your salon is in a cold area, you can offer a free take-home moisturizing conditioner with each color service.

FEBRUARY was my favorite time of year to put promotional packages together. I would make packages for both men and women with Valentine's Day in mind. I would make packages with men's products for the wife to buy, and vice versa. I made little baskets with kids shampoo, conditioner and gels, and I would put candy hearts all over the basket. These were always a huge winner.

MARCH & APRIL bring spring, and Easter was such a fun time to create packages for kids and parents. I would design kid's packages with chocolate eggs, jelly beans and some of our favorite children's hair products such as color gels.

I would have the staff show these to our mothers and fathers to entice them to buy.

I also made adult baskets with candy and plastic eggs that contained a surprise percentage off their next visit.

I would shrink wrap moisturizing shampoo and conditioner, and I would make baskets with makeup for mom and baskets of men's gel and body wash for dad.

In MAY, Mother's Day has always been a traditional celebration of appreciation for the best mothers in the world. Gift certificates and a variety of shrink- wrapped retail products were always winners.

JUNE is Father's Day, and we would do the same.

In the SUMMER time, I would decorate my salon with summer, beach theme. I would put products together with beach towels and leave-in conditioners to protect the hair from the sun. I would also put together clarifying shampoo and treatments for the swimmer to cleanse salts or chlorine out of the hair.

In addition, I would put packages together geared for the skin to protect it from the sun.

AUGUST was the perfect time to promote back to school hairstyles that are gorgeous and easy to maintain.

I filled little plastic lunch boxes with children's products for back to school.

For junior high, high school, and college-aged clients, I would create a package of age-appropriate make up and skin care to add a natural fresh look.

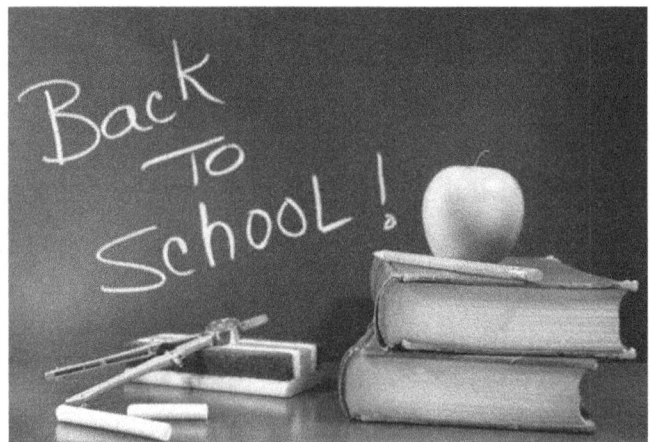

In August, we also did very well with liter sales, usually by offering 2 liters for $20.00 that we normally sold for $35.00. They flew off the shelf.

FALL was a great time to promote rejuvenation for tired, dull hair. Often times, chlorine, sun, and salt water will really damage the hair and skin when not protected carefully. I offered in-salon deep protein conditioner treatments along with a hydrating moisture mask.

Fall is also a great time for salons to run a color service promotion, cross merchandising with home maintenance products. This will encourage the client to purchase professional products that will keep the hair in a healthy state. For example, with every color service you get 25% off any product of your choice.

In NOVEMBER it is time to get ready for the holidays and to create holiday package promotions.

Gift certificates, stocking stuffers, and gift baskets should be the center of attention in your salon. You can also cross promote up-do services with manicures, pedicures, and facials. A one-stop shop is very popular, where the client can get several services at a great promotional price.

- Another tool that is great for any time of year is the wonderful incentive program I mentioned earlier in this workshop which utilizes vacation certificates as an incentive to encourage clients to spend more in your salon. It is a value added strategy that is a complete winner. When I discussed them earlier, I mentioned I used these certificates as performance incentives for my staff.

- The certificates are great for clients too. Y o u c a n give your clients vacation certificates as a reward for purchasing services and products at your salon. Your existing clients will have an incentive to return more frequently and spend more money. You will attract new clients and generate referrals, too, because who wouldn' t want a free 3 day/2 night hotel stay! Please visit my website at www.PositiveSalonStrategies.com to learn more about vacation vouchers.

Again, the ideas are endless. Be creative and have fun!

In summary, there are seven simple rules of retailing for salon professionals to remember that will help them begin to retail successfully. Teach your stylists the following:

1. Remember you are serving the client NOT selling to her.

2. Find common interests with your client during the consultation. This will send the message that you find this person interesting enough to engage in conversation, and it will create a bond between you.

3. Listen to the tone, tempo, and speed in which your client is speaking and try and match it.

4. If a client says she does not want to buy a product, it most often means that she does not have enough information or she doesn' t understand what you are trying to relay to her. Herein lies a great opportunity to educate your client.

5. Take all the information that you receive from your client during the consultation and use this knowledge to suggest a variety of ser- vices that may interest her.

6. Keep in mind that making powerful recommendations will increase your service and retail sales.

7. Remember something that good wait staff know: They are likely to receive higher tips when they make knowledgeable suggestions to their customers about food and drinks that are on the menu. It shows they know their business.

I have taught these rules of retailing for years and have used them with the staff in my own salons as well.

I know that all the proven tips we have covered in this book work, and I also know that you will be successful when you implement them into your clients' consultations and during the time you are servicing your clients too.

Remember that retailing should be a part of each salon ser- vice. Putting a solid plan in action to increase your retail sales should be a crucial component of your business plan. Retail sales can account for incredibly increased profits. You want your retail sales to pay your bills and that should be one of your business goals.

Retailing in Action Worksheet

Do you carry products that motivate and excite your staff? Yes_____No_____

Do you offer product training to all members of your staff? Yes_____No_____

Do your stylists use your salon's products? Yes_____No_____Some_____

Do you send products home regularly with your stylists so they can become personally familiar with all the products' benefits and features? Yes_____No_____

Do you talk with your stylists about what products they like and what products they don't like? Yes_____No_____

Do you involve your entire team when deciding what products to carry? Yes_____No_____

Do you work with companies that provide product education training for your staff? Yes_____No_____

What stylist retailing incentives do you use?

_____

_____

_____

_____

Are your products displayed neatly and attractively? Yes_____No_____Somewhat_____

Do you change your displays regularly? Yes_____No_____Not as often as I should_____

Do you dress up your windows and change the displays with the seasons and/or holidays? Yes_____No_____

Do you utilize complimentary tools and materials from your product companies? Yes_____No_____

What type of product satisfaction guarantee do you, or will you, provide for your customers?

_____

_____

_____

_____

My action plan for creating promotional packages to help my stylists stay focused on selling retail and to increase my retail sales will be:

_____

_____

_____

_____

AdditionalThoughts:

_____

_____

_____

_____

_____

_____

_____

_____

_____

_____

_____

Sample of Texture Menus:

TEXTURE DESIGN MENU

Making Waves

Luxurious alternating wave pat- terns that move in the direction that best suits your hair.

Bodifying or Volumizing Treatment

Amplify the fullness and thickness of your hair texture with- out adding curl.

Style Support

Texture to create life and volume at the base of the hair shaft to support the finished design.

Structurizing

Define your hair style by adding silky, voluminous texture. By alternating the size and direction of curl, you enhance shape and add dimension to your hair style.

The Design Direction

As individual as you are, this texture technique follows the design lines of your desired hair style to create a low maintenance, easy-care yet fashionable finish.

Spiral Texture Service

From loose spiraled formations to coiled ringlets of curl, the results are soft, feminine and creative.

Zonal or Partial Waves

A technique of adding partial support or hidden movement only in the design areas that require added texture treatment.

Texture a la Carte

Texture – where you need it or want it. Add a few waves in those problem areas for style, support, or personalized effects.

Sample of Texture Menus:

TEXTURE TREATMENT MENU

Curl Reducer Treatment

Change the wave pattern of natural curls or relax too tight or curly hair.

Curl Straightener Treatment

Remove all natural waves and curls for shiny and silky straight hair styles. Treat perm re- growth and straighten to natural state as hair is growing out.

Hair Softening Treatment

Re-texture coarse, wiry hair to a soft and manageable texture.

Directional Texture

Redesign hair growth patterns by taking control of cowlicks and neck line patterns or change wave patterns in specific areas, like the fringe.

CHAPTER FOUR

STYLISTS ARE BUSINESS OWNERS TOO

STYLISTS ARE BUSINESS OWNERS TOO

SECTION ONE

YOUR CHAIR <u>IS</u> YOUR BUSINESS!

Welcome to the chapter , "Stylists are Business Owners Too!" Stylists often fail when they do not think of their chair and styling station as their own. In this segment I will review the importance of treating your styling station as if it were your own business.

In chapter one, I will teach you the tricks and techniques to be successful behind the chair and will go over the importance of image, outstanding customer service, cleanliness, and being updated technically on all the newest trends.

In this chapter , although it is titled "for new stylists," I offer a step-by-step guide for any salon professional on how to find the right salon that would be a great fit for you. Although this workshop is geared for stylists, there is a place for the owner too, as I offer suggestions to help the salon owner help their stylists achieve their best. I so enjoy sharing this information with you, so let's get started!

Perhaps you've just graduated cosmetology school and you're ready to hit the floor, or you just moved across the country and you don't know a soul, or you are presently at a salon where you need to build a more solid customer base, or you have chosen to be a booth renter. Whatever the reasons you have for needing to make it a top priority to build your clientele, this workshop will help you to become the best entrepreneur ever.

Before you start to market for clients, define what type of client you want in your chair. Take some time. Write down a description of your ideal client. Include age, taste in hairstyles and lifestyles as part of your description. The more detailed your description, the easier it will be for you to determine how to build your clientele:

Once you have written goals on the type of client you will target, then if you are not currently at a salon, you will need to determine the type of salon and atmosphere in which you wish to work.

I a l w a y s encourage a stylist who is looking for a salon to go in first as a customer to get a feel for the place. Think like a client. Is the customer service great, are the stylists dressed professionally, and is it a place in which you would be proud to work? Choose a location that will provide built-in ways to get new clients. For example, a mall is a great place to work if you are new to the area because it has a lot of traffic. Ask, and make sure, a salon is actively pre-booking appointments, offers on- going education, and has a hands-on owner or manager who believes in doing promotions on a monthly basis. This indicates the shop cares about bringing in new clients - and retaining them. I go into this job search process in more detail in chapter three.

But for now, let's assume you are working in a salon and have been successful in building a clientele. Now you must keep those clients coming back to YOU. You are competing not only with outside salon businesses, but you are also competing with stylists within your salon.

This is why it is so important to differentiate yourself from the rest of the staff. In doing this, though, you must remember to always maintain a team-member mentality.

So the first step is to take the time to go over some very important questions that I would like you to answer carefully. You will use this questionnaire to re-evaluate your business and get it on the right track.

- Is your chair making you money? Yes No_ If not, you need to look at all the ideas we go over in this workshop and re-evaluate your business.

- Is your station clean and orderly? Yes   No   No one wants to sit in clutter and have you use dirty tools.

- Are you pampering, pampering, and pampering your clients? Yes   No If you are not, someone else will. A client will continue to return to a place where she is made to feel good inside and out.

- Do you have impeccable customer service skills? Yes___No___ Poor guest service is a main reason why a client will not return. If you are not making your client feel like she is the most valuable being alive, someone else will.

- Are you up to date on all the newest trends and technical skills? Yes No On-going education is critical for all stylists in order to stay on top of their game. Keeping updated allows you to be able to introduce new and trendy styles to your clients. It is so important that you know how to duplicate a specifi style when your client wants her hair to look like her favorite celebrity.

- Are you always professionally dressed, with make-up applied, and your hair styled fashionably? Yes   No   You can't expect to sell fashion and beauty to your client if you are not sporting it yourself. A client will be attracted to the stylist who i s dressed professionally, with clean, styled hair and tastefully applied makeup.

- Are you prepared for your clients? Do you offer on-time service? Yes No We all run behind schedule at one time or another. Clients really appreciate it when they are not made to wait for their appointments. However, if you happen to run late, make sure your client is comfortable waiting with something to drink and read.

- Ask yourself, would you want to sit in your chair if you were the client? Yes___No___ Always look at your station through the eyes of a customer. Make sure your station is clean and orderly for each client no matter how busy you get. No one wants to sit down in a chair with hair in it and look down to see hair all over the floor. Your combs and brushes should be cleaned and disinfected after each use.

- Are you dependable and flexible with your clients? Yes___No___ When I was working behind the chair, I made it a point to stay late or come in early for my clients when it was necessary. This is especially important when building a loyal clientele. I always tried to accommodate the client that had an unexpected dinner or other engagement to go to and needed me to squeeze her in to do her hair for the event. It's just good business.

- Do you show passion and enthusiasm for your work? Yes___No___ There is nothing worse than to have a stylist who seems bored and who doesn't seem to want to be at work. I tell stylists they must treat their profession like a career and not like a dull job they go to each day to collect a pay check. Your clients will be able to tell, and they won't come back to you. If you are feeling in a rut, try talking to someone you feel comfortable with (perhaps your salon owner or manager), and ask for suggestions. You might consider taking a motivational class to tap into your passion again. And always, always invest in on-going education. It helps to keep you motivated and will give you fresh ideas to offer your clients.

- Are your delivering the highest quality and predictable results to your customers? Pampering your clients and offering exceptional customer service are crucial when building a loyal clientele, but so is delivering outstanding end results. You must be able to address your client's hair needs accurately and give her the style and look that is the best it can be. So keep yourself updated on the newest trends and keep yourself technically trained on all haircuts and chemical services.

- Again, I bring this up because it is important:

- Is your position as a stylist your career or just a job? Career_____ Job _____

It is so important for stylists to view their position as a career where they have chosen a specific path, have received the proper training, and are then willing to keep updated all the time.

Make sure you have gone through all of these questions and have answered them thoroughly one by one. Be honest when answering and be ready to change the things that will put you on top of your game.

Next, we want to probe a little bit deeper with a few more questions. Write down as much information as you can so that you will be able to build a realistic plan going forward.

_____

_____

_____

_____

Describe your present situation. For example, what type of money are you making? How strong is your customer base? Is your retention of clients good, or is it the best?

_____

_____

_____

_____

Now write down where you want to be. For example, I want to be making x amount of money so I can purchase a car, a house, etc.

_____

_____

_____

_____

Next, jot down the changes you would like to implement in your business. Keep in mind that once you put all this information together, you should plan to start by doing it one change at a time. No need to overwhelm yourself. The first mile of a journey is taken with the first step.

_____

_____

_____

_____

Now, armed with all of the information you have gathered in these pages of questions we have covered, it is time to create an action plan and to put a strategy in place to strengthen the areas that need improvement.

So write an action plan stating how you can be more successful in building and retailing a solid clientele. Here are some examples. I need to keep my styling station cleaner. I need to take some motivational classes so I feel more inspired in my job.

I need to be more proactive in taking control of my business in order to grow my customer base.

My action plan will be

_____

_____

_____

_____

_____

_____

_____

You will find specific business building suggestions throughout the rest of the workbook.

Now let' s continue to probe a little deeper and see how you perceive yourself.

I am a firm believer that we eventually become what we think. Negative thinking will affect the way you view yourself and others. I have lived by the statement, whatever comes after the thought or words "I am " is exactly what you will become. For example, if you tell yourself, "I am talented," then the chances are, you will be talented! But on the other hand if you tell yourself, "I am uncreative," then the chances are you won' t even try tasks that you feel require creativity.

Negative thinking emits negative energy. A client can feel when there is friction with staff and when the salon has negative energy. I have witnessed situations where clients would not go back to a salon for the sole reason that they felt so uncomfortable with the way the staff treated each other.

So remind yourself that the mind is like a garden. You need to weed out all the negative and polluted thinking and replace it with positive affirming thoughts. Otherwise the weeds will choke out all the beautiful things that could grow.

You also have to remember that you cannot control anyone else's behavior but your own. Don't get caught up in senseless gossip or fall into the negative trap. And most importantly, leave your personal problems at the door when you arrive at work.

To be a complete success, you can't just rely on your boss. Self-promotion is so important whether you are the new kid on the block or have been working in the salon for years. I made it a practice to hand out my business card to everyone I met - in restaurants, night clubs, grocery stores, etc. I used to volunteer to work at fashion and bridal shows, and I used to do makeovers for local news anchors in order to get noticed.

Once you have established a growing customer base, start asking for their help in bringing you their friends and family.

Let them know you are looking for new customers and promise to reward them if they help you.

A method that always worked for me

was referral cards. Give each client three to five of your business cards and have your client put his or her name on the back. When all of those cards have come back to the salon in the hands of new clients, give your original customer a free service or product.

Let's talk more about having a Successful Referral Program.

You can either use your business cards as I described above, or you can order pre-printed referral cards. If you use the preprinted referral cards, here is how I suggest you do it:

1. Fill in the referral cards with the salon's name and your name and information. Place these cards in a clear acrylic holder at YOUR station.

2. At the end of every service, give each of your clients three referral cards. Explain to them that when they refer a friend who brings in the referral card, the new client and the existing client will both receive a special gift. Tell them to

be sure to fill out the card with their name and address and to do the same for the person they are referring.

3. Each time a new client comes in with a referral card, present her with the gift of your choice—a free product, an add-on service, a discount, etc. You can fill in the blank with your choice of gift.

4. I always mailed a gift certificate postcard to clients who referred their friends to me to use toward their next service. Don' t forget to make the certificate valid for a specific period of time, such as 30 days. This will encourage clients to book their next appointment right away in order to use their gift certificate postcard, before it expires, and get their discount.

It doesn' t take a rocket scientist to know that clients are stretching out the time between appointments. But what you may be surprised to learn is how much money you' re losing when clients don' t return every six weeks. In a down economy, pre-booking is a sure winner.

I had huge success getting my clients to pre-book early, and I will share with you how I did that.

First, you will need to determine the gift you will be providing to clients when they pre-book their next appointment. Make sure it' s a gift that will build your business, such as a retail product, a complimentary add-on service, or dollars off their next service.

Consider changing it up every few months.

Next, you, the stylist, should make out your own cards with your name and the reward you have decided to give that client. Then, make sure to place your pre-

book cards on your station where they are visible. You may even want to put up a cute card on your mirror saying, "Ask me how you can save money on your next appointment." If you forget to mention the cards, the client will most likely ask how.

Remember, you want to reward your clients for getting back into your chair before they even leave it.

Consider using punch cards too. They are a great way to get clients back into your chair. Punch cards are catching on in many retail businesses. And why not? Everyone is looking for deals, so why not reward your clients for coming to see you for services and for buying their retail in your salon.

In my salons I created two different punch cards, one for services and one for retail products.

Here's how you do it:

1. First, establish the value of each punch hole.

2. Next, establish the value of a fully punched card. For example, will you offer a free service or free retail product once the card is fully punched?

3. Place the cards in acrylic holders at your station.

4. After a service or retail purchase, fill in the client's name, the value for each punch, the award for a completed punch card, and the expiration date. Present a completed card to every client.

5. Once services are rendered or retail is purchased, punch the card for your client.

6. Each time your client returns, ask for her punch card. Don't count on the receptionist to do this for you.

7. Once the card is filled with punches, award the gift for a completed card.

Okay, so what happens if you can't afford to get these different cards? Why not try teaming up with other stylists and splitting the costs? Obviously, it will be more cost efficient than getting them printed yourself. This will also generate excitement amongst the staff.

So stylists, find a way to utilize these various card programs. Your customers will feel appreciated and rewarded which, in turn, will entice them to become the town crier on your behalf!

STYLISTS ARE BUSINESS OWNERS TOO
SECTION TWO

A SPECIAL NOTE FOR NEW STYLISTS

So you have made it through school with flying colors, and now you are ready to hit the real world!

In this chapter, I will offer some suggestions to help you find the right job for you, and I will help you prepare to be a huge success. Get ready to put together a simple business plan that will assist you in getting organized and help you find a salon that will be a nice fit for you.

Although this guide has been written with new graduates in mind, the information I offer is beneficial for any salon professional at any stage in his/her career.

My first suggestion is for you to make a list of things that you should discover about a salon that would entice you to work at that specific salon. The best way to do this is to visit the salons that you are interested in applying to as a customer, first, before you schedule an interview. As a customer, how do you feel about the salon and the staff? For example, do the stylists get along, and do they work together well as a team? Is the customer service impeccable? Are the stylists and front desk staff friendly and accommodating? Is the salon clean and inviting? Is the atmosphere friendly, and does the salon exude warmth? Are the technical skills of the stylists who are doing hair current and up-to-date? Another question you should ask yourself is do you want to work in a full-service salon or a salon that offers just haircuts and styles?

List the things that are important to you in a salon in which you would consider working:

_____

_____

_____

_____

_____

_____

_____

I suggest that brand new, graduating stylists not apply at high- end salons and end up working as an assistant. So many times I have seen stylists lose their technical skills because they are doing only shampoos and occasional blow-dries. Clients tend to label these new stylists as assistants and don' t always give them the chance to be a stylist for them. Instead, I would suggest starting at a chain salon that offers full train- ing and on- going education and that also does lots of advertising to help stylists to build their clientele.

So now you have narrowed down your list to salons that you would love to work in, and you have set up an interview with the manager and owner, but first, you must make another plan.

Make a list of all the things that you need to discuss with the owner or manager.

- For example, does the salon only offer booth rentals? Booth rentals are not good for someone right out of school because a booth renter must have an established clientele in order to benefit from being a booth renter.

- Will you be an employee paid hourly or will you be paid on commission only? Starting out as a new stylist, being paid hourly is best. You need time to build a clientele and no matter what percentage you are offered, 50% of 0 is 0. Wait a year and then revisit it.

- Does the salon offer on-going advanced education? On-going education is very important for stylists to stay updated and current.

- Does the owner offer incentive programs for the stylists?

- Incentive programs are important because incentives allow the stylist to stay motivated, they create excitement in the salon with the clients and staff, and they provide a great way to earn extra money. Stylists are more apt to remain at a salon where they are motivated, happy, and earning extra money!

- What does the owner expect of his/her employees? It is so important that you know what the owner's expectations are and what your job description will be.

- For example, does the owner require you to retail a certain percentage of sales each week, and does the owner require a certain production per hour for your service sales? It benefits both the stylist and the owner to have a clear understanding of the owner's expectations so that the stylist can determine if he/she is comfortable with those expectations.

- What types of benefits does the salon offer? For example, health insurance, paid holidays, paid ongoing educational classes, etc.

- What are the work shifts like? If you have limitations on when you can work this has to be addressed upfront in the interview.

- What type of goals are set for you by the salon? For example, are you expected to retail, and if so, is there a separate commission for retail? The ideal situation is where the salon offers an additional commission for retail above and beyond your regular pay.

- Is there an orientation period to help you transition into your first real job? Ideally you should be offered a period of orientation because it will help you to familiarize yourself with the salon and the staff. I used to have a buddy system where my new stylist would work closely with my manager or a senior stylist for about one month. At that point, mos new stylists were comfortable with their surroundings and knew where to find all the tools and supplies necessary for work, so they are comfortable enough to do just fine on their own.

List the items you want to discuss during a salon interview:

_____

_____

_____

_____

Remember that the more information you find out about a salon, the staff, and their policies ahead of time, the more likely you are to find a salon that is a good fit for you. Also, remember that hopping from salon to salon is not good for your career. So, do your homework ahead of time, and note that it takes time (a good year anyway) to build a clientele. So be prepared to stay at the salon you chose and give it a chance!

It is always so exciting to begin a new opportunity. Enjoy this time, make it count for all it's worth, and I wish you success!

ABOUT THE AUTHOR

Jeanne Degen is a leader in the beauty industry. For 33 years, she has brought her expertise to salons, manufacturers and distributorships as an educator, a trainer, a stylist and as a successful salon owner. Now she has created Positive Salon Strategies, a salon consulting company that delivers easily accessible, proven business strategies to salon professionals in the beauty profession.

Her 10-minute online workshops are designed as easy to follow, step-by- step instructional programs that allow salon professionals to learn effective techniques for business success. The workshops feature tips and strategies that Jeanne herself used to manage and grow her salon business. She knows how hectic running a salon can be, and she is confident and excited that the short format instruction provided by Positive Salon Strategies will help others to be more successful at operating their businesses.

Jeanne brings impressive professional experience to bear in her company. As Director of Operations and Education at Fantastic Sam's International Corp, she has assisted franchisees nationwide to build salon revenue. She not only offered education and operational support to established salons, but also supervised and conducted new salon opening trainings, including interviewing and hiring new staff. She has taught and created workshops that address employee turnover, that motivate staff to sell, create winning salon promotions, power re- tailing, and that help create great customer service, among many other topics. Jeanne also consulted with salon owners and franchisees on profitability, inventory control, client retention, and all business aspects necessary for operating a successful salon.

Jeanne has also held positions at internationally acclaimed companies, including various beauty Distributors, National Director of Education at ISO and National Education and Sales Manager at Helene Curtis. She has hands-on stylist experience and has performed platform work with some of the most elite platform artists in the industry. Most importantly, Jeanne is thrilled to realize her dream of supporting the growth and prosperity of the salon community through her company, Positive Salon Strategies.

www.ingramcontent.com/pod-product-compliance
Lightning Source LLC
Chambersburg PA
CBHW080315220326
41519CB00071B/7149